A-LEVEL

G000019500

FLASH NOTES

EDEXCEL YEAR 2

New Syllabus 2015

Dr C. Boes

Condensed Revision Notes (Flashcards) for
Successful Exam Preparation

Designed to Facilitate Memorization

For corrections, comments and special offers go to:

www.alevelchemistryrevision.co.uk

Table of Contents

Paper 1 – Advanced Inorganic and Physical Chemistry (9CH0/01) 7

Topic 11 Equilibrium II 7
Equilibrium & Gas Equilibrium 7
Example Calculations - Gas Equilibrium 9

Topic 12 Acids-Bases Equilibria 11
Strong Acids and Bases 11
Weak Acids 13
Buffers 15
Buffer Example Calculations 17
Titration Curves I 19
Titration Curves II 21

Topic 13 Energetics II 23
Born-Haber Cycle 23
Enthalpy Change of Solution 25
Entropy 27
Free Energy 29

Topic 14 Redox II 31
Electrode Potentials 31
Redox Equations 33
Calculating Voltages of Cells & Applications of Cells 35
Redox Titrations 37
Example Calculation – Redox Titration 39

Topic 15 Transition Metals 41
Transition Elements 41
Complexes 43
Stereoisomerism in Transition Metal Complexes 45
Reactions of Transition Metal Ions 47

Paper 2 – Advanced Organic and Physical Chemistry (9CH0/02) 49

Topic 16 Kinetics II 49
Rate of Reaction 49
Rate Constant k & Rate Determining Step 51
S_N1 and S_N2 Mechanisms for Haloalkane Hydrolysis 53
Concentration-Time Graphs & Half-Life 55
Rate-Concentration Graphs 57
Iodine Clock 59
Arrhenius Equation 61

Topic 17 Organic Chemistry II 63
Optical Isomers 63
Aldehydes & Ketones 65
Carboxylic Acids 67
Esters 69
Acyl Chlorides 71

Topic 18 Organic Chemistry III 73
Benzene & Arenes..73
Reactions of Arenes 75
Phenol..77
Amines..79
Preparation of Amines & Amides...81
Condensation Polymers...83
Amino Acids & Proteins 85
Preparation and Purification of Organic Compounds 87
Extending Carbon Chain Length 89

Topic 19 Modern Analytical Techniques II...91
NMR Spectroscopy: H-NMR & Carbon 13-NMR 91
How to predict NMR Spectrum from Structural Formula 93
Thin Layer Chromatography & Mass Spectroscopy.........................95
Gas Liquid Chromatography & HPLC 97
Organic Synthesis, Functional Groups & Combined Techniques...99

Appendix: Periodic Table of Elements 101

How to use these notes

These revision notes are organized in chapters according to the current 2015 Edexcel Year 2 syllabus (from Sept 2015). Each chapter contains individual revision cards covering all the necessary topics. Everything in *italic* is optional knowledge, aimed at students who want to excel or want to continue with chemistry at university. **Bold** represents important keywords or key definitions. 'Data sheet' indicates information which will be provided on the data sheet or in the question during the exam and does not need to be memorized. Important information and exam-specific tips are highlighted in yellow.

How to memorize: The revision cards are introduced by their titles and keywords on a separate page. After reading the title you should try to write down the content of the card without looking at the next page. The keywords give you hints about the content. Write down everything you remember, even if you are not sure. Then check if your answers are correct; if not, rewrite the incorrect ones.

At the beginning, when you are still unfamiliar with the cards, it might help to read them a few times first. If they contain a lot of content, you can cover the revision card with a piece of paper and slowly reveal the header and sub content. While you uncover it try to remember what is written in the covered part, e.g. the definition for a term you just uncovered. This uncovering technique is for the early stages, later you should be able to write down the whole content after just reading the header. If this is the case, move to the next card. If not, bookmark the card and memorize it repeatedly. Do at least four to five sessions per week until you know all the cards of one chapter word-perfectly. When you have memorized a revision card apply your new knowledge by answering topic questions. Then move on to the next section. Generally it is better to do shorter sessions more often than longer sessions less frequently. An even better option is to ask somebody to check your knowledge by reading the header aloud and comparing your answer to the content.

Exam techniques

Begin with a quick look through the exam. How is it structured; what topics are coming up and how many questions are there? Then work systematically through it from the beginning, but keep an eye on the time. When you fall behind shorten your answers and leave difficult topics for the end.

Underline or highlight the important information/data in the question. If just names for compounds are given, write the chemical formula above it (e.g. sulfuric acid -> H_2SO_4).

Circle the functional groups in an organic formula and name them. Draw the carbons and hydrogens in skeletal formulae or displayed formulae if the structural formulae are given.

Make sure you read the question thoroughly and be aware what actions are expected from you from the command words used.

Identify the topic of the question and mentally bring up the flashcards associated to the topic. They will help you with the answer. If you have problems understanding the question, read it again slowly and also read through the follow up sub-questions (a, b, c etc.) sometimes the topic and the initial question becomes clearer. If you still do not understand the question or cannot come up with all the answers, do not spend any more time on it. Write down your best answers or just standard keywords/phrases from the flashcard. Writing something is better than writing nothing. You might still get some marks for it. Circle the question and come back to it at the end of the exam.

If you do calculations, write down a list of the data given (time permitting – otherwise just underline) and the formulae/equations which you are using (even if your calculation is wrong, you might get a mark for the correct formula).

Always show your workings and do the unit calculations. This means writing the units next to the numbers and cancelling or multiplying them accordingly. You should get the correct unit for your final answer. If not, you might not have converted them correctly (e.g. cm^3 into dm^3) or have used the wrong equation.

After writing down the final answer check if it makes sense (is the number in the expected range; does it have the correct sign in front, e. g. – for an exothermic reaction etc.).

Calculation answers should always be given in decimals, never fractions. Furthermore make sure you have answered all the questions and everything asked for (e.g. state symbols, significant figures etc.)

For multiple choice questions: read all answers and strike through the ones which are definitely wrong. Choose the correct or most likely of the remaining ones. If you have no clue take the longest answer. Always choose an answer -> you have at least a 25 % chance to get it right :-).

Do not spend too much time on a question. Rule of thumb is 1 min per mark. If you are unsure, circle the question and come back to it at the end of the exam.

More tips about how to plan your revision and how to prepare for exams can be found on my website: https://www.alevelchemistryrevision.co.uk

Disclaimer: Due to the changing nature of mark schemes it cannot be guaranteed that answering according to these notes will give you full marks. These notes constitute only one part of a full revision program and work alongside other methods, like practising past papers. They have been created with great care; however, errors or omissions cannot be excluded. They are designed for the final stage of revision and require a thorough understanding of the topics.

Paper 1 – Advanced Inorganic and Physical Chemistry (9CH0/01)

Topic 11 Equilibrium II

Equilibrium

&

Gas Equilibrium

Properties of equilibrium constant k (four points)

Equation for total pressure of gas mixture

Equation for mole fraction

Equation for partial pressure

Equation for Equilibrium constant K_p

Properties of K_p (two points)

Equilibrium

-> see Year 1 revision card 'Equilibrium and Reversible Reactions'

Equilibrium constant K_c (for aqueous system)
- K_c only temperature dependent
- when temperature is increased then K_c increases for endothermic reactions and decreases for exothermic reactions
- If concentration of [C] or [D] is increased *(numerator)*, concentrations of [A] and [B] must also increase *(denominator)* to keep K_c constant (equilibrium moves to the left)
- Solids (and liquids) do not appear in the equilibrium equation

Gas Equilibrium

The total pressure of a gas mixture is the sum of all partial pressures of the individual gases

$p_{total} = \Sigma p_{partial}$

p: pressure [atm]

Partial pressures can be calculated from mole fractions:

Mole fraction $\chi = \dfrac{\text{n (one gas)}}{\Sigma \text{n (all gases)}}$ n: moles [mol]

$\qquad\qquad\qquad\qquad\qquad\qquad$ *χ: Greek letter chi*

$p_{partial} = \chi \times p_{total}$

Equilibrium constant K_p can be calculated from partial pressures:

$$aA_{(g)} + bB_{(g)} \leftrightarrows cC_{(g)} + dD_{(g)}$$

$$K_p = \frac{p(C)^c \, p(D)^d}{p(A)^a p(B)^b}$$

K_p : equilibrium constant
p: partial pressure [atm]

- **only temperature dependent => see Year 1 revision card**
- **liquids and solids do not appear in the equilibrium equation of a heterogeneous system**

Example Calculations - Gas Equilibrium

Example Calculations Gas Equilibrium

Example I

PCl_5 is thermally decomposed at 350 C

$$PCl_5 \rightleftharpoons PCl_3 + Cl_2$$

The gas mixture at equilibrium contains following gases with these partial pressures:
partial pressure of Cl_2 $p_{partial}$ = 250 kPa
partial pressure of PCl_3 $p_{partial}$ = 250 kPa
partial pressure of PCl_5 $p_{partial}$ = 178 kPa

What is the total pressure of this gas mixture?

p_{total} = (250kPa + 250 kPa + 178 kPa)
      = **678 kPa**

Example II

-> see also Year 1 revision card 'Equilibrium Concentrations Calculations'
-> highlight all data given (**bold**) in the question and write down mole ratios
-> create a table as specified below

3.0 moles of PCl_5 have been thermally decomposed in a sealed container. The equilibrium mixture contains **1.75 mol of chlorine gas**. The **total pressure is 678 kPa**. Calculate the partial pressure of PCl_5.

$$PCl_5 \rightleftharpoons PCl_3 + Cl_2$$

	PCl_5	PCl_3	Cl_2
Initial moles n_i	**3.0**		
Equilibrium moles	1.25	1.75	1.75

All mole ratios: 1:1

Equilibrium moles of reactant (PCl_5): $n_{er} = n_i - x$ = 3.0 – 1.75 = 1.25

Σ n (all gases) = (1.75 moles + 1.75 moles + 1.25 moles) = 4.75 moles

Mole fraction χ (PCl_5) = $\dfrac{1.25 \text{ moles}}{4.75 \text{ moles}}$ = 0.263

$p_{partial}$ (PCl_5) = χ x p_{total} = 0.263 x 678 kPa = 178 kPa

---

Topic 12 Acids-Bases Equilibria

Strong Acids and Bases

pH-Definition

Calculate pH of strong acid

Monoprotic and diprotic acids

Tip

Acid strength depends on...

Conjugated acid-base pairs

Ionic product of water

Equation for calculating pH of strong base

Chemical formula of hydronium ion

pH scale

How to measure pH

Maths

Strong Acids & Bases

pH-Definition:

$$pH = -\log_{10}[H^+]$$

pH of strong acid:

$$pH = -\log_{10}[H^+]$$

=> **[H$^+$] equals concentration of the acid e.g. HCl**, unless it is a diprotic acid, like H_2SO_4, which has double the H$^+$ concentration

Monoprotic (monobasic): $HCl \rightarrow H^+ + Cl^-$
Diprotic (dibasic): $H_2SO_4 \rightarrow 2H^+ + SO_4^{2-}$

> -> If the strong acid is neutralised with a strong base, subtract the moles of OH$^-$ from the initial moles of H$^+$ before calculating the resulting pH

The stronger the ability of an acid to donate protons, the stronger the acid
-> for **reactions of acids** see Year 1 revision card 'Acids'

An acid can become a base if paired with a stronger acid, forming new **conjugated acid-base pairs**:

$$HNO_{3(l)} + H_2SO_{4(l)} \leftrightarrows H_2NO_3^+{}_{(l)} + HSO_4^-{}_{(l)}$$
     base1   acid2   acid1   base2

H_2SO_4/HSO_4^- are a conjugated acid-base pair (linked by an H$^+$-transfer)

Ionic product of water:

$$H_2O \leftrightarrows H^+ + OH^- \qquad \text{(slightly dissociated)}$$

$k_w = [H^+] \times [OH^-] = 10^{-14} \, mol^2 \, dm^{-6}$ *at 25 °C*   *(data sheet)*

=> increases with temperature increase (endothermic bond breaking)

pH of strong base:

$$pH = 14 + \log[OH^-]$$

=> **[OH$^-$] equals concentration of the base** e.g. NaOH, unless it is a dibasic base like $Ca(OH)_2$, which has double the OH$^-$ concentration

H$^+$ forms H_3O^+ (hydronium ions) with water

pH scale: acidic < 7 neutral < alkaline

pH can be measured with pH-meter or indicator strips

Maths:
$0.001 = 1 \times 10^{-3}$ -> **use standard form for scientific calculations**
$\log 1 \times 10^{-3} = -3$
$\log \sqrt{} = \frac{1}{2}$
$\log (x \cdot y) = \log x + \log y$

Weak Acids

Equation for dissociation of weak acid

Equilibrium constant equation

Neutralization enthalpies for strong and weak acid

How to calculate the pH of a weak acid

Two assumptions

Equation to calculate H^+ concentration of a weak acid

Definition of pK_a

The larger pK_a ....

Example calculation

Weak acid (Practical)

$$HA \rightleftharpoons H^+ + A^-$$

$$K_a = \frac{[H^+][A^-]}{[HA]}$$

K_a: acid dissociation constant [mol dm^{-3}]
-> the larger K_a, the stronger the acid (more dissociation, higher [H$^+$])
[HA]: acid concentration at equilibrium [HA]$_{eq}$

The enthalpy change of neutralisation is less exothermic for weak acid than strong acids, because energy is used up for the acid dissociation

Calculate pH of weak acid:

1st assumption: $[A^-] = [H^+]$ (neglects H_2O dissociation)
2nd assumption: $[HA]_{eq} = [HA]_{initial}$ (neglects HA dissociation)
        -> only valid if dissociation is negligible e.g. K_a is relatively small

Rearrange equilibrium constant equation towards [H$^+$]:

$$[H^+] = \sqrt{(K_a \times [HA])}$$

$$pH = \frac{1}{2}(pk_a - log\,[HA]) \qquad \text{(-log of the equation above)}$$

pK$_a$

$$pk_a = -log\,K_a$$

the larger pk_a, the weaker the acid (similar to pH), e.g. chloric(I) acid HClO (pk_a 7.4) weaker acid than ethanoic acid (pK_a 4.8)

Example calculation

Calculate the pH of 0.0010 M (mol dm^{-3}) methanoic acid (K_a = 1.6 x 10^{-4} mol dm^{-3})

$$K_a = \frac{[H^+][A^-]}{[HA]}$$

$$[A^-] = [H^+]$$

$$[HA]_{eq} = [HA]_{initial}$$

$[H^+]^2 = k_a \times [HA]_{initial}$ = 1.6 x 10^{-4} mol dm^{-3} x 0.001 mol dm^{-3}
          =   1.6 x 10^{-7} mol^2 dm^{-6}

$[H^+]$ = $\sqrt{1.6 \times 10^{-7}}$ mol^2 dm^{-6} = 4 x 10^{-4} mol dm^{-3}

pH = -log [H$^+$] = -log 4 x 10^{-4} = **3.4**

Buffers

General definition of buffer

Definitions of acidic and basic buffers

Two methods of buffer preparations

Workings of a buffer

pH-calculation for buffer with two assumptions

Tip

Blood buffer with equation (three points)

Buffers

Definition: A solution that minimizes pH changes on addition of small amounts of acid or alkali.

A buffer is an aqueous mixture of a weak acid and its salt (conjugate base) in
high concentrations -> acidic buffer   *or*
Mixture of weak base and its salt -> **basic buffer**

Preparations

I) Mix a weak acid and its salt ($CH_3COOH + CH_3COONa$)   *or*

II) Mix excess weak acid with a limited amount of strong alkali (NaOH)
   -> salt is formed during the neutralization reaction
   => make sure to use the buffer equation and not the weak acid equation to calculate the pH in an exam question.

Workings of a buffer

$$NaA \rightarrow Na^+ + A^-$$

$$HA \leftrightharpoons H^+ + A^-$$

Adding H^+:   system moves to the left: A^- removes H^+ by forming HA
Adding OH^-: OH^- removes H^+ by forming water; system moves to the right: **HA** dissociates, replacing H^+

Calculate pH:

$$[H^+] = K_a \times \frac{[HA]}{[A^-]}$$

$$pH = pk_a + \log\frac{[A^-]}{[HA]}$$ *Henderson-Hasselbalch equation*

[A^-]:   concentration of salt (base)   **Assumption:** salt fully dissociated
[HA]:   concentration of acid   **Assumption:** $[HA]_{eq} = [HA]_{initial}$

-> If [HA] = [A^-] then pH = pk_a

pH range of buffers: pk_a +/- 1

Blood buffer:

$$H_2CO_3 \leftrightharpoons HCO_3^- + H^+$$

- pH 7.35 – 7.45 controlled by **carbonic acid/hydrogen carbonate buffer**
- **Acidosis:** H^+ increases, shift to the left, forming H_2CO_3
  H_2CO_3 decomposes into H_2O and CO_2, which is breathed out and blood pH returns to normal
- **Kidneys** control HCO_3^- levels

Buffer Example Calculations

Buffer Example Calculations

I) What is the pH of a buffer, after mixing **100 cm^3 0.10 mol dm^{-3}** ethanoic acid with **300 cm^3 0.20 mol dm^{-3}** sodium ethanoate?

pk$_a$ (ethanoic acid) = 4.77, K$_a$ = 1.7 x 10^{-5} mol dm^{-3}

Calculation:

Final volume: 100 cm^3 + 300 cm^3 = 400 cm^3

c (CH$_3$COOH) = (0.1 dm^3 x 0.1 mol dm^{-3}) / 0.4 dm^3 = 0.025 mol dm^{-3}

c (CH$_3$COONa) = (0.3 dm^3 x 0.2 mol dm^{-3}) / 0.4 dm^3 = **0.150 mol dm^{-3}**

$$pH = pka + log \frac{[A^-]}{[HA]}$$

$$pH = 4.77 + log \frac{0.150}{0.025}$$

$$pH = 5.6$$

II a) What is the pH of a buffer, after mixing propanoic acid and propanoate ions with final **concentrations of 1.00 mol dm^{-3}** for both?

b) What is the pH after **6.90 g** of **Na** have been added to 1.00 dm^3 of this buffer?

K$_a$ (propanoic acid) = 1.35 x 10^{-5} mol dm^{-3}

a) pH = pka = -log 1.35 x 10^{-5}

pH = 4.87

b)   Na + CH$_3$CH$_2$COOH -> CH$_3$CH$_2$COONa + ½H$_2$

n(Na) = 6.9 g / 23 g mol^{-1} = 0.30 mol

Mole ratios: Na : HA : A$^-$ 1 : 1 : 1

In 1 dm^3:

n(CH$_3$CH$_2$COOH) = 1.00 mol – (0.30 mol) = 0.7 mol   (- HA removed)

n(CH$_3$CH$_2$COO$^-$) = 1.00 mol + (0.30 mol) = **1.3 mol**   (+ A$^-$ produced)

Divide by volume (1 dm^3) to get concentrations for [HA] and [A$^-$]

$$pH = pka + log \frac{[A^-]}{[HA]} = 4.87 + log \frac{1.3}{0.7}$$

$$pH = 4.87 + 0.269$$

$$pH = 5.14$$

Titration Curves I

Characteristics of titration curves (three points)

Graph strong acid/strong base

Graph weak acid/strong base (three points)

Half-equivalence point

Titration curves I

Titrations -> see year 1 revision card 'Titrations'

- **area around equivalence point has to be drawn as a straight vertical line**
- start and end point of the curve have to match the pH of the solutions used: need to calculate pH from the data given
- the pH of indicator colour change must match the equivalence point

Strong Acid / Strong Base

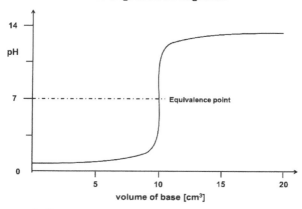

-> **any indicator**

Weak Acid / Strong Base

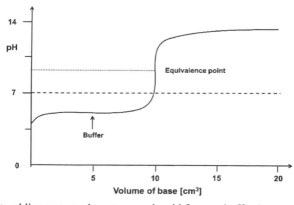

-> adding a strong base to a weak acid forms a buffer (see revision card)
-> phenolphthalein (colourless -> pink)
-> equivalence point above 7 because the salt produced is alkaline

Half-equivalence point: Half of the acid has been neutralized (here at 5 cm^3)
- **pH = pka** of weak acid: [HA] = [A$^-$] => cancel out in equilibrium equation

Titration Curves II

Graph strong acid/weak base (two points)

Graph weak acid/weak base (one point)

How to record titration curves

Titration curves II

Strong Acid / Weak Base

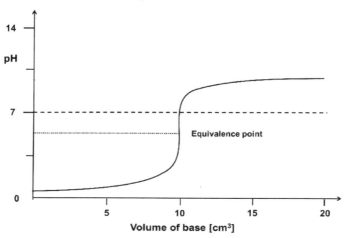

-> methyl orange (red -> yellow)
-> equivalence point below 7 because the salt produced is acidic

Weak Acid / Weak Base

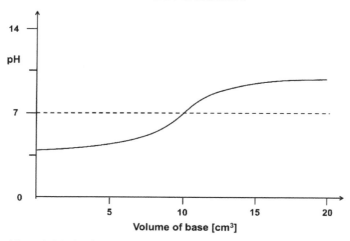

-> Not suitable for titration with indicator (no significant pH-jump)

To record titration curves, increasing volumes of the standard solution are added with a burette and the pH is continuously measured with a pH meter (needs to be calibrated).

Topic 13 Energetics II

Born-Haber Cycle

Purpose

Definition of lattice enthalpy

Characteristics of lattice enthalpy (three points)

Equation for lattice enthalpy

Example with different enthalpies and equations

Tip

Polarisation of ions with definition (four points)

Born-Haber Cycle

-> to calculate lattice enthalpy of a salt (application of Hess's law)

Lattice enthalpy

Definition: Energy given off when **gaseous ions** form **1 mole** of an **ionic solid** (salt) under standard conditions. (always negative)

- to estimate the strength of bonds in an ionic compound (salt)
  -> determines it's physical characteristics (solubility, melting point)
- higher charge, smaller ions -> stronger electrostatic attraction => increase of lattice enthalpy
- often cannot be measured (very exothermic) -> indirect approach => Born-Haber splits the process of forming a salt from its elements (standard states) in small steps, which can be measured or calculated

$$\text{Hess's law:} \quad \Delta H^{\ominus}_{latt} = \Delta H^{\ominus}_{f} - \Delta H^{\ominus}_{others}$$

$\Delta H^{\ominus}_{latt}$:   standard lattice enthalpy
$\Delta H^{\ominus}_{f}$:   standard enthalpy of formation
$\Delta H^{\ominus}_{others}$: Σ enthalpies transforming elements into gaseous ions:
    atomisation + ionisation + affinity enthalpies

Example:

$$Na_{(s)} + \tfrac{1}{2} Cl_{2(g)} \text{ -> } NaCl_{(s)}$$

$\Delta H^{\ominus}_{at}$: **standard enthalpy of atomization** $Na_{(s)} \text{ -> } Na_{(g)}$

E_{I1}:   **first ionization energy** $Na_{(g)} \text{ -> } Na^{+}_{(g)} + e^{-}$
    => only remove one mole of electrons at a time (1st and 2nd ionisation), never 2 moles

$\Delta H^{\ominus}_{at}$: **standard enthalpy of atomization** $\tfrac{1}{2} Cl_{2(g)} \text{ -> } Cl_{(g)}$

E_{aff}:   **electron affinity** $Cl_{(g)} + e^{-} \text{ -> } Cl^{-}_{(g)}$
    First electron affinity is exothermic: $O_{(g)} + e^{-} \text{ -> } O^{-}_{(g)}$
    Second affinity endothermic (e^{-} to O^{-} repel) $O^{-}_{(g)} + e^{-} \text{ -> } O^{2-}_{(g)}$

$\Delta H^{\ominus}_{latt}$:   **standard lattice enthalpy** $Na^{+}_{(g)} + Cl^{-}_{(g)} \text{ -> } NaCl_{(s)}$

-> memorize Year 1 revision card 'Enthalpy changes - Definition'

$$\Delta H^{\ominus}_{latt} = \Delta H^{\ominus}_{f} - \Delta H^{\ominus}_{others}$$

$$\Delta H^{\ominus}_{latt} = \Delta H^{\ominus}_{f} - (\Delta H^{\ominus}_{at}[Na_{(s)}] + E_{I1}[Na_{(g)}] + \Delta H^{\ominus}_{at}[Cl_{(g)}] + E_{aff}[Cl_{(g)}])$$

Make sure you multiply $\Delta H^{\ominus}_{at}$ and E_{aff} by two for salts with formula MX_2

Polarisation of ions
-> is the distortion of its electron cloud (away from completely spherical)
- A cation has polarising power and will distort an anion.
  higher charge, smaller cations (charge density) -> stronger polarising power
- An anion is polarisable: the larger the easier it is polarized (size alone)
- The more polarisation the more degree of covalent bond (stronger) instead of ideal ionic bond
=> explains why experimental lattice energies (Born-Haber) are higher than theoretical ones (Coulomb's law, ideal ions)

Enthalpy Change of Solution

Definition of enthalpy change of solution
Equation for enthalpy change of solution
Energetic conditions for a salt to be soluble (two points)

Definition of enthalpy change of hydration
Characteristics of hydration enthalpy (three points)
Equation to calculate enthalpy change of hydration
Calculate hydration enthalpies from single ions
Example calculation

Enthalpy change of solution $\Delta H_{solution}$

Definition: Enthalpy change when 1 mole of a substance is completely dissolved under standard conditions

Dissolving consists of two competing processes:
1) hydration of ion releases energy (exothermic -)
2) breaking up the lattice requires energy (endothermic +)

$$\Delta H_{solution} = \Delta H_{hyd} - \Delta H_{latt}$$

The lattice enthalpy ΔH_{latt} (energy released when salt formed) is exothermic (-), therefore sign in front of ΔH_{latt} becomes positive (-- = +)

=> $\Delta H_{solution}$ must be negative ($\Delta H_{hyd} > \Delta H_{latt}$) or slightly positive (due to increased entropy) for a salt to be soluble

-> use Gibbs equation to calculate if salt is soluble at a given temperature (see revision card 'Free Energy')

Enthalpy change of hydration ΔH_{hyd}

Definition: Enthalpy change when 1 mole of gaseous ions form aqueous ions (dissolve) under standard conditions

- increases with **charge density** of ion (smaller ion, higher charge)
- exothermic: electrostatic attraction between ion and dipole water
  -> **ion-dipole bonds**
- it is a theoretical value (gaseous phase), but can be calculated with the equation below (Hess's law), since $\Delta H_{solution}$ can easily be measured:

$$\Delta H_{hyd} = \Delta H_{solution} + \Delta H_{latt}$$

- **add hydration enthalpies of each ion to get hydration enthalpy of the whole salt:**

$$\Delta H_{hyd} (CaCl_2) = \Delta H_{hyd} (Ca^{2+}) + 2 \times \Delta H_{hyd} (Cl^-)$$

Example

Calculate if $CaCl_2$ is soluble in water, by using the data below.
$\Delta H_{hyd}(Ca^{2+})$:   -1579 kJ mol^{-1}
$\Delta H_{hyd}(Cl^-)$:   -364 kJ mol^{-1}
$\Delta H_{latt}(CaCl_2)$:   -2255 kJ mol^{-1}

$$\Delta H_{solution} = \quad \Delta H_{hyd} \quad - \quad \Delta H_{latt}$$
$$\Delta H_{solution} = [-1579 + (2 \times -364)] - (-2255) \qquad | \text{ kJ mol}^{-1}$$
$$\Delta H_{solution} = \qquad -52 \text{ kJ mol}^{-1}$$

=> $\Delta H_{solution}$ is negative, therefore $CaCl_2$ should be soluble in water

---

Entropy

Definition

Entropy depends on... (three points)

Equation for ΔS_{sys} with rule

If entropy increases then sign for ΔS is...

Equation for ΔS_{total}

Equation for ΔS_{surr}

Tip

Equation for free energy and equilibrium constant

Example

Entropy

Definition: Randomness or disorder of a system

Entropy depends on:
I) Physical State: solid < liquid < gases
-> increasing freedom of movement & disorder
=> increasing entropy (positive)
II) Temperature: increasing temperature -> increasing entropy
III) Number of Moles: Increasing number of moles -> increasing entropy

Entropy change in a chemical reaction

$$\Delta S_{sys} = \Sigma S_{prod} - \Sigma S_{react}$$

ΔS_{sys}:   entropy change of the reaction [J K^{-1} mol^{-1}]
S: molar entropies (of products or reactants)

-> Multiply S by mole numbers from mole-equation

If the system loses energy by increasing the entropy then the sign in front of $+\Delta S$ is positive -> contrary to the negative sign in front of exothermic reactions: $-\Delta H$

-> Entropy is a form of energy

Total entropy change of reaction

$$\Delta S_{total} = \Delta S_{sys} + \Delta S_{surr}$$

-> includes entropy of surroundings (ΔS_{surr}) in an open system (energy exchange with surroundings)

$$\Delta S_{surr} = - \frac{\Delta H}{T}$$

T: temperature in Kelvin (0 °C = 273 K)
ΔH: enthalpy change of reaction [J mol^{-1}] **(often given in KJ -> convert!)**

Free Energy and Equilibrium Constant

$$\Delta G = -RT \ln K$$

R: gas constant 8.31 J K^{-1} mol^{-1}
ln K: natural log of equilibrium constant
-> the larger K the more feasible the reaction (K > 1)

Example:

$$2NO_{2(g)} \leftrightarrows 1N_2O_{4(g)}$$

S (N_2O_4):   304 J K^{-1} mol^{-1}
S (NO_2):   240 J K^{-1} mol^{-1}

$\Delta S_{sys} = 304 - (2 \times 240) = -176$ J K^{-1} mol^{-1}
-> decrease of entropy because of fewer gas moles on product side

---

Free Energy

Gibbs equation

Tip

For a reaction to occur spontaneously ΔG must be....

To calculate temperature for spontaneous reaction set ΔG to...

Different combinations of exothermic/endothermic ΔH with ΔS

A reaction with negative ΔG might not happen due to....

Example calculation

Free energy

Gibbs equation

$$\Delta G = \Delta H - T\Delta S_{sys}$$

ΔG: free energy change of the system (reaction) [J mol^{-1}]
ΔH: enthalpy change of the reaction [J mol^{-1}] **(often given in KJ -> convert!)**
ΔS_{sys}: entropy change of the reaction [J K^{-1} mol^{-1}]
T: temperature [Kelvin]

=> ΔG must be negative for reaction to occur spontaneously

-> set $\Delta G = 0$ to calculate minimum temperature for spontaneous reaction

- For an exothermic reaction (-ΔH) and a positive ΔS: TΔS adds to the free energy value because the sign before TΔS stays negative
- For an exothermic reaction and negative ΔS: TΔS subtracts from the free energy value because the sign becomes positive (+ TΔS)
- For an endothermic reaction (+ΔH) and positive ΔS: TΔS subtracts from the energy value (If T$\Delta S > \Delta H$ then ΔG becomes negative: an endothermic reaction can happen spontaneously)
- **-> A reaction with negative ΔG still might not happen spontaneously due to slow kinetics (high activation energy)**

Example Calculation

Calculate the free energy change of the following reaction at room temperature under standard pressure.

$$NH_{3(g)} + HCl_{(g)} \leftrightarrows NH_4Cl_{(s)}$$

ΔH_f (NH$_3$):   -44 kJ mol^{-1}
ΔH_f (HCl):   -94 kJ mol^{-1}
ΔH_f (NH$_4$Cl)   -310 kJ mol^{-1}

S(NH$_3$):   188 J K^{-1} mol^{-1}
S(HCl):   190 J K^{-1} mol^{-1}
S(NH$_4$Cl):   98 J K^{-1} mol^{-1}

$\Delta H_r^{\ominus} = -310 - (-44 + -94) = $ **-172 kJ** mol^{-1}

$\Delta S^{\ominus}_{sys} = 98 - (188 + 190) = $ -280 J K^{-1} mol^{-1}

$$\Delta G = \Delta H - T\Delta S$$
$$\Delta G = -172,000 \textbf{ J} - (298 \text{ K} \times -280 \text{ J K}^{-1} \text{ mol}^{-1})$$
$$\Delta G = -88,560 \text{ J mol}^{-1}$$

=> The reaction will be spontaneous because ΔG is negative

At a higher temperature ΔG might become positive and the reaction will not happen spontaneously anymore.

Topic 14 Redox II

Electrode Potentials

Definition of standard electrode potential

Standard hydrogen half-cell with conditions (five points)

Diagram of electrochemical cell with hydrogen half-cell

Five rules for electrode potential

Three rules for cell diagrams with example

Electrode Potentials (Practical)

Standard electrode potential $E^\ominus$
Definition: Voltage of a half-cell measured against a standard hydrogen half-cell, under standard conditions

Standard hydrogen half-cell: 1M HCl, 298K, 100 kPa H_2 ($Pt|H_2|H^+||$ ...)
- the voltage ($E^\ominus$) of the standard hydrogen half-cell is **defined as 0V**
- other half-cell contains **1 M ion solution** and is connected by salt bridge
- when two ions form a half-cell (Fe^{2+}/Fe^{3+}) **platinum** is used as an **electrode**
- electrode potentials express the tendency to lose or gain electrons
- ions move through **salt bridge ($KNO_{3(aq)}$)** to complete circuit and to maintain charge balance.

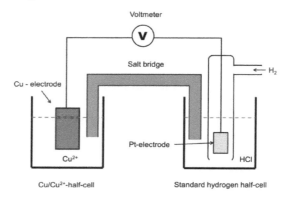

Cu/Cu²⁺-half-cell   Standard hydrogen half-cell

Rules for electrode potential
1) **The greater the tendency of a metal to lose electrons (being oxidized) the more negative the potential (more reactive)**
2) Half-equations are always written as equilibrium with double arrows *(sometimes single arrows in exams/literature due to typeset limitations)*
3) By convention, half reactions of electrochemical cells are always written as a reduction process (species with more positive oxidation number first).
$$Cu^{2+} + 2e^- \leftrightharpoons \quad Cu$$
(This does not apply to half equations of normal Redox equations)
4) Potential depends on temperature and concentration (or pressure for gases)
5) **A change of concentration or pressure (gases) which increases the number of electrons (e^-), makes the potential more negative**

Rules for Cell Diagrams
1. Write half-cell with the more negative potentials first *($E^\ominus Cu/Cu^{2+}$: 0.34 V)*
2. Oxidised forms (ions) go in the middle next to double lines (salt bridge)
3. Write inert electrodes (Pt) always on the outside
4. Example: $Pt \mid H_2 \mid H^+ \parallel Cu^{2+} \mid Cu$

Redox Equations

How to combine half-equations (six points)

Predicting redox reactions – circling method (four points)

Example

Prediction can be wrong (two points)

Redox Equations

Combine half-equations to produce full (ionic) equations
- write the half equations in the correct direction as forward reactions (oxidation/reduction according to $E^{\ominus}$)
- use oxidation states to determine the number of transferred electrons
- number of electrons **transferred must be the same for the full equation**
- multiply both half-equations to get the lowest common multiple (here: 6)
- cancel everything which appears on both sides of the equations, e.g. electrons, H^+, H_2O etc. (here: electrons)
- to combine to a full equation, add all remaining reactants ($2Fe^{3+}$, $3Zn$) and products ($2Fe$, $3Zn^{2+}$) together on their respective sides.

$$Zn \;\rightarrow\; Zn^{2+} + 2e^- \qquad\qquad |\; x\, 3$$
$$Fe^{3+} + 3e^- \;\rightarrow\; Fe \qquad\qquad\quad |\; x\, 2$$
$$\underset{0}{3Zn} + \underset{+3}{2Fe^{3+}} \rightarrow \underset{0}{2Fe} + \underset{+2}{3Zn^{2+}}$$

$$H_2O_2 \;\rightarrow\; O_2 + 2H^+ + 2e^-$$
$$H_2O_2 + 2H^+ + 2e^- \;\rightarrow\; 2H_2O$$
$$\underset{+1\;\;-1}{2H_2O_2} \;\rightarrow\; \underset{0}{O_2} + \underset{+1\;-2}{2H_2O}$$

Predicting direction of redox reaction (checking if a redox pair can react)
a) half-equation with more negative potential loses electrons (oxidation); more positive potential gains electrons (reduction)
b) highlight (bold arrows) the direction of the reaction according to potential and circle reactants required *(example below: Zn/Zn^{2+} has lowest potential and reaction goes to the left to lose electrons, hence Ag/Ag^+ goes to the right).*
c) see if the reactants are present on the left side of the overall reaction equation to decide if the pair of compounds can react (feasible)
d) if the reaction is feasible, write 'E_{cell} is positive (+)', if not negative (-)

Example
Would the reaction $Zn^{2+} + 2Ag \rightarrow Zn + 2Ag^+$ happen?

$$Zn^{2+} + 2e^- \;\rightleftharpoons\; \boxed{Zn} \qquad\qquad E^{\ominus} = -0.76 \text{ V}$$
$$\boxed{Ag^+} + e^- \;\rightleftharpoons\; Ag \qquad\qquad E^{\ominus} = +0.80 \text{ V}$$

Answer: No, because according to their potentials only Zn and Ag^+ (circled) could react and they are not the reactants in the overall equation.
With Zn^{2+} and Ag as reactants, the E_{cell} would be negative -> not feasible

Prediction can be wrong
- Non standard conditions: change of temperature or concentration -> equilibrium shifts to a side increasing/decreasing $E^{\ominus}$ (Le Chatelier)
- Rate of reaction too slow (activation energy too high)

Calculating Voltages of Cells

&

Applications of Electrochemical Cells

Equation to calculate E_{cell}

E_{cell} always...

E_{cell} proportional to...

Applications of Electrochemical cells (two points)

Three cell types with properties and examples

Electrode reactions for lithium cell

Electrode reactions for alkaline hydrogen-oxygen fuel cell

Electrode reactions for acidic hydrogen-oxygen fuel cell

Other application

Calculating Voltage of Electrochemical Cell (Electromotive force: EMF)

$$E_{cell} = E_{higher (Red)} - E_{lower (Ox)}$$
-> always positive

E_{cell} proportional to ΔS_{total} and $\ln K$ (K: equilibrium constant)

Applications of Electrochemical Cells

- The potential difference between two electrochemical half cells creates an electromotive force (EMF) in an electrochemical cell
- This force is able to drive electrical devices like mobile phones & tablets

Cell types

- **Batteries – non rechargable** (irreversible reactions)
  e.g. alkaline batteries (Zn/C)
  -> cheap, last longer but create more waste

- **Storage Cells – rechargeable** (reversible reactions)
  e.g. rechargeable batteries like Lithium- or Ni/Cd cells
  -> more power, saves money over time, less waste but toxic & expensive

- **Fuel Cells:** creates a voltage through the reaction of a fuel ,e.g H_2 (or methanol), with oxygen: hydrogen-oxygen fuel cells
  -> no recharging, no toxic waste (H_2O), (no direct CO_2 emission), more efficient than combustion, but H_2 is explosive, difficult to store and needs energy to produce (fossil fuel)

Lithium Storage Cell
Negative electrode (-): $Li \rightarrow Li^+ + e^-$
Positive electrode (+): $Li^+ + CoO_2 + e^- \rightarrow Li^+[CoO_2]^-$
Overall: $Li + CoO_2 \rightarrow Li^+[CoO_2]^-$

Alkaline Hydrogen-Oxygen Full Cell
Negative electrode (-): $2H_2 + 4OH^- \rightarrow 4H_2O + 4e^-$
Positive electrode (+): $2H_2O + O_2 + 4e^- \rightarrow 4OH^-$
Overall: $2H_2 + O_2 \rightarrow 2H_2O$

Acidic Hydrogen-Oxygen Full Cell
Negative electrode (-): $H_2 \rightarrow 2H^+ + 2e^-$ |x2
Positive electrode (+): $O_2 + 4H^+ + 4e^- \rightarrow 2H_2O$
Overall: $2H_2 + O_2 \rightarrow 2H_2O$

Other application
- **Corrosion prevention**: zinc coating for iron products prevents rusting

---

Redox Titrations

General characteristics (five points)

Three reaction equations

Working through a redox titration question (five points)

Redox Titration (Practical)

- Is used to determine the concentration of a substance which can be oxidized or reduced
- Needs a suitable indicator, which is difficult for redox reactions (ideally one of the reactants/products changes colour e.g. potassium manganate (VII) purple -> pink/colourless)
- No big jump at the equivalence point as with pH titration
- The endpoint is reached, when the solution in the flask takes on the colour of the solution in the burette (unless an indicator, e.g. starch, is used)
- Often I_2/starch complex (dark blue) is used as an indicator (blue colour disappears or shows up). This might require a second redox reaction

Reactions used in redox titrations

MnO_4^- $_{purple}$ $+ 8H^+ + 5e^-$ -> Mn^{2+} $_{colourless\ (pink)}$ $+ 4H_2O$ (only with H_2SO_4 dilute)

Fe^{2+} -> $Fe^{3+} + e^-$

$I_{2\ blue} + 2e^-$ -> $2I^-$ $_{colourless}$

Working through a Redox titration question

- Circle or highlight all data given in the exam question
- Write the dilution/volume ratio and molar ratios on the side of the mole equations
- Work backwards, starting with calculating the number of moles of standard solution used in the actual redox titration from its concentration and volume
- Use the molar ratios and dilution ratios for step by step backwards calculations, as shown in the example calculation (a - e)
- Strike through the ratios after they have been used in the calculation

-> For general redox terms and rules see Year 1 revision cards

Example Calculation – Redox Titration

Redox Titration - Example Calculation

5.0 g of hydrated copper(II) sulphate, $CuSO_4 \cdot XH_2O$, was dissolved in 50 cm^3 **of water**. Iodide was added in excess and reacted with the Cu^{2+}-ions, forming iodine as described in equation (1). A 5 cm^3 **portion** of the solution, with the produced iodine, was taken and titrated with **0.10 M sodium thiosulphate** solution, with starch as the indicator (equation 2). The endpoint was reached when the blue colour disappeared. The volume of thiosulphate solution used was **20 cm^3**, as measured with a burette. How many moles (X) of water of crystallisation does the hydrated copper sulphate contain?

1. Reaction: Forming I_2
An excess of I⁻ solution is used to completely reduce the Cu^{2+} ions, whose concentration we want to determine. The moles of Cu^{2+} ions are directly proportional to the moles of I_2 produced in a 2:1 ratio.

(1) $2Cu^{2+} + 4I^- \rightarrow 2CuI + I_2$ (2:1)

2. Reaction: Titration of I_2 with thiosulphate standard solution (known concentration)
                                                                (1:10)

(2) $2S_2O_3^{2-} + I_2 \text{ (blue)} \rightarrow 2I^- \text{ (colourless)} + S_4O_6^{2-}$ (2:1)

From the volume of thiosulphate used, we can calculate the number of moles of I_2 and subsequently the number of moles/concentration of Cu^{2+} and water of crystallisation:

Steps

a) Calculate the number of moles of sodium thiosulphate used in the titration
$n = cV$ $= 0.1$ mol dm^{-3} 0.02 dm^3 $= 0.002$ mol

b) Calculate the number of moles of Iodine molecules in the 5 cm^3 portion
2:1 ratio: 0.002 mol / 2 = 0.001 mol

c) Calculate the number of moles of Iodine molecules in the 50 cm^3 original solution
1:10 ratio: 10 x 0.001 mol = 0.01 mol

d) Calculate the number of moles of copper ions in 5.0 g of hydrated CuSO$_4$
2:1 ratio: 2 x 0.01 mol = **0.02 mol**   = moles of anhydrous CuSO$_4$

e) Calculate the moles of water of crystallization (X) in hydrated copper (II) sulphate
-> see Year 1 flashcard 'Water of Crystallisation'

$M_r (CuSO_4) = 63.5 + 32.1 + 4\text{x}16 = 159.6$ g/mol

$m = nM = 0.02$ mol x 159.6 g mol^{-1} = 3.192 g CuSO$_4$ (anhydrous)

m (H_2O) = 5 g − 3.192 g = 1.808 g

n (H_2O) = 1.808 g / 18 g mol^{-1} = **0.100 mol**

$X = \dfrac{0.1 \text{ mol}}{0.02 \text{ mol}} = 5$

The Chemical formula of the hydrated copper (II) sulphate used in this experiment was
$CuSO_4 \cdot 5H_2O$

Topic 15 Transition Metals

Transition Elements

Definition

Two d-block elements which are not transition metals

Order of filling the subshells

Two elements with special electron configurations

Where the colour comes from (including one equation)

Colour changes happen due to... (three points)

Properties of their oxidation states & naming (three points)

Applications as catalysts (four points)

They form...

Reason for their properties

Four oxidation states of Vanadium with colours

Transition Elements

Def.: Transition elements have a partially filled d subshell in at least one ion

General Characteristics

- **Sc, Zn not transition metals**: Sc^{3+} and Zn^{2+} do not behave like transition metals -> these ions have an empty or full d-subshell => **colourless**
- **4s filled first and removed before 3d** (4s lower energy than 3d)
- **Electron configuration Cr [Ar] $3d^5$ $4s^1$, Cu [Ar] $3d^{10}$ $4s^1$**
  -> half full and completely full d subshells are more stable => **colourless**
- Coloured compounds:
  -> ligands split d-orbital into two energy levels
  -> e^- can be excited to a higher level by absorbing light ($\Delta E = h\nu$)
  -> remaining light is reflected and responsible for the colour
  Colour changes happen due to changes in:
  -> oxidation states
  -> coordination number
  -> ligand
- Oxidation number is written as roman numerals, in brackets in the salt name, e.g. Iron(II) sulphate: $FeSO_4$, Iron(III) sulphate: $Fe_2(SO_4)_3$
- High oxidation state -> **oxidising agent**
- Low oxidation state -> **reducing agent**
- Good **heterogeneous catalysts** because of their **variable oxidation states** and **weak surface interactions** between reactant and 3d/4s electrons (Fe -> ammonia, V_2O_5 -> sulphuric acid, Ni -> hydrogenation) -> see Y1 'Catalyst'
- **Fe^{2+} catalyses** reaction between iodide and persulphate ions
  I) $S_2O_8^{2-} + 2Fe^{2+}$ -> $2SO_4^{2-} + 2Fe^{3+}$
  II) $2I^- + 2Fe^{3+}$ -> $2Fe^{2+} + I_2$
- **Mn^{2+}** (product) **auto-catalyses** reaction between MnO_4^- and $C_2O_4^{2-}$ ions
- Good **homogenous catalyst** because of **variable oxidation states** and functioning as **oxidising/reducing agents**
- They form **complexes** (see revision card 'complexes')
- Many of their properties are due to their **unfilled d orbitals**

Oxidation states of Vanadium

VO_3^-	(+5)	white solid ($NH_4VO_3 + H^+$ -> yellow solution, see below)
VO_2^+	(+5)	yellow solution
VO^{2+}	(+4)	blue solution
V^{3+}	(+3)	green solution
V^{2+}	(+2)	violet solution

-> these successive oxidation states are achieved by adding Zn to acidic vanadium(V) solution. Zn acts as reducing agent -> Zn^{2+}

Complexes

Definition of complex

Definition of ligands

Monodentate etc.

Definition of coordination number

Shapes (five points)

Ligand exchange (three points and three equations)

Test for water with equation

How to write chemical formulae of complexes (two points)

Haemoglobin (three points)

Complexes (Practical)

Terms

Complex: Central metal atom/ion + ligands

Ligands: form **dative covalent bonds to metal ion**

Monodentate, bidentate (Ethan-1,2-diamine; $C_2O_4^{2-}$), **multidentate** (EDTA): number of dative bonds from **one** ligand

Coordination number (x): number of bonds between metal and ligands

Shapes

- linear (2), e.g. $[Ag(NH_3)_2]^+$
- tetrahedral/square planar (4)
- octahedral (6)
-> small ligands (H_2O, NH_3) are usually 6-coordinate (octahedral)
-> large ligands (Cl^-) usually 4-coordinate (tetrahedral)

Ligand exchange

- product complex usually more stable $(K_{stab} > 1)$
- polydentate complex more stable than monodentate (H_2O, Cl^-)
-> entropy increases due to more product molecules => *chelate effect*
- can lead to change in coordination number

$[Cu(H_2O)_6]^{2+}_{(aq)}$ blue $+ 4NH_3 \leftrightarrows [Cu(NH_3)_4(H_2O)_2]^{2+}$ **deep-blue** $+ 4H_2O$

$[Cu(H_2O)_6]^{2+}_{(aq)}$ blue $+ 4Cl^- \leftrightarrows [CuCl_4]^{2-}$ yellow $+ 6H_2O$

$[Cr(H_2O)_6]^{3+}_{(aq)}$ green $+ 6NH_3 \leftrightarrows [Cr(NH_3)_6]^{3+}$ **violet** $+ 6H_2O$

Test for H_2O

Cobalt paper: $[CoCl_4]^{2-}_{(aq)}$ blue $+ 6H_2O_{(l)}$ -> $[Co(H_2O)_6]^{2+}_{(aq)}$ pink $+ 4Cl^-_{(aq)}$

Chemical Formulae

- square brackets are used for complex-formulae (and concentrations)
- **overall charge of complex** = charge central ion + sum of charges of ligands

Haemoglobin

- a complex of Fe^{2+} with porphyrin and globin protein
- the sixth ligand is O_2
- CO binds more strongly than O_2 => Poisoning *(asphyxiation)*

Stereoisomerism in Transition Metal Complexes

Optical isomerism with example (draw)

Cis-trans Isomers with three examples

Cis-platin with application (draw)

Stereoisomerism in Transition Metal Complexes

Optical Isomerism *(Enantiomers)*

Octahedral complexes with bidentate ligands form two optical isomers:

$[Ni(H_2NCH_2CH_2NH_2)_3]^{2+}$ (Ethan-1,2-diamine – "en")

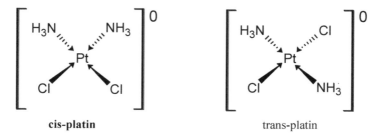

-> **need to be able to draw structures**

-> see revision card 'Optical Isomers'

Cis-trans Isomerism

Square planar and octahedral complexes with at least **two pairs of monodentate ligands** show cis/trans isomerism:

$[Ni(NH_3)_2Cl_2]$ *square planar*

$[CoCl_2(NH_3)_4]^+$ octahedral (trans: Cl opposite, cis: Cl adjacent)

$[Pt(Cl)_2(NH_3)_2]$ square planar

cis-platin   trans-platin

-> **cis-platin is anti-cancer drug:** binds to DNA and prevents cell division
-> see Year 1 revision card 'Types of Isomers'

Reactions of Transition Metal Ions

Four Chromate reactions

Six metal-aqua Ions with colours

Acidity with two equations and three points

Five Precipitation reactions with NaOH/NH$_3$-solutions

Two amphoteric reactions of Cr^{3+}

Three further reactions with ammonia

Reactions of Transition Metal Ions

Chromate Reactions

Reduction of Dichromate(VI) with Zn/HCl

$Cr_2O_7^{2-}$ $_{orange}$ $+ 14H^+ + 3Zn \rightarrow 2Cr^{3+}$ $_{green}$ $+ 7H_2O + 3Zn^{2+}$

$Cr_2O_7^{2-}$ $_{orange}$ $+ 14H^+ + 4Zn \rightarrow 2Cr^{2+}$ $_{blue}$ $+ 7H_2O + 4Zn^{2+}$

Oxidation of Cr^{3+} with H_2O_2 under alkaline conditions

$2[Cr(OH)_6]^{3-}$ $_{green}$ $+ 3H_2O_2 \rightarrow 2CrO_4^{2-}$ $_{yellow}$ $+2OH^- + 8H_2O$

Chromate/Dichromate Equilibrium

$2CrO_4^{2-}$ $_{yellow}$ $+ 2H^+ \leftrightarrows Cr_2O_7^{2-}$ $_{orange}$ $+ H_2O$ acid-base reaction

Metal-Aqua Ions

$[Cu(H_2O)_6]^{2+}$	blue
$[Fe(H_2O)_6]^{2+}$	green
$[Co(H_2O)_6]^{2+}$	pink
$[Fe(H_2O)_6]^{3+}$	yellow
$[Cr(H_2O)_6]^{3+}$	green
$[Cr(H_2O)_6]^{2+}$	blue (after reduction of Cr^{3+} with Zn)

Acidity

$[M(H_2O)_6]^{2+} + H_2O \leftrightarrows [M(H_2O)_5(OH)]^+ + H_3O^+$

$[M(H_2O)_6]^{3+} + H_2O \leftrightarrows [M(H_2O)_5(OH)]^{2+} + H_3O^+$

- **hydrolysis** of water
- weak acidic for M^{2+}
- stronger acidic for M^{3+} -> greater polarising power (charge/size ratio)

Test for Transition Metals (Practical)
Precipitation reactions with NaOH or NH_3-solutions *(simplified equations)*

Co^{2+} $_{(aq)}$	pink	$+ 2OH^-$ $_{(aq)}$	$\rightarrow Co(OH)_{2(s)}$	blue precipitate
Cu^{2+} $_{(aq)}$	blue	$+ 2OH^-$ $_{(aq)}$	$\rightarrow Cu(OH)_{2(s)}$	blue precipitate
Fe^{2+} $_{(aq)}$	pale green	$+ 2OH^-$ $_{(aq)}$	$\rightarrow Fe(OH)_{2(s)}$	green precipitate
Fe^{3+} $_{(aq)}$	yellow	$+ 3OH^-$ $_{(aq)}$	$\rightarrow Fe(OH)_{3(s)}$	**orange-brown/rust prec.**
Cr^{3+} $_{(aq)}$	green	$+ 3OH^-$ $_{(aq)}$	$\rightarrow Cr(OH)_{3(s)}$	green precipitate

Amphoteric (reacts with acids and bases):

$Cr(OH)_{3(s)}$ $+ 3OH^-$ $_{(aq)}$ $\rightarrow [Cr(OH)_6]^{3-}$ $_{(aq)}$ excess OH^- => green sol.

$[Cr(OH)_3(H_2O)_3]_{(s)}$ $+ 3H^+$ $_{(aq)}$ $\rightarrow [Cr(H_2O)_6]^{3+}$ $_{(aq)}$ dissolved in acid

Further reactions with NH_3

$Co(OH)_{2(s)}$ $+ 6NH_3$ $\rightarrow [Co(NH_3)_6]^{2+}$ $_{(aq)}$ $+ 2OH^-$ $_{(aq)}$ yellow sol.

$Cr(OH)_{3(s)}$ $+ 6NH_3$ $\rightarrow [Cr(NH_3)_6]^{3+}$ $_{(aq)}$ $+ 3OH^-$ $_{(aq)}$ **purple sol.**

$[Cu(OH)_2(H_2O)_4]_{(s)}$ $+ 4NH_3$ $\rightarrow [Cu(NH_3)_4(H_2O)_2]^{2+}$ $_{(aq)} + 2H_2O_{(l)} + 2OH^-$ $_{(aq)}$

blue precipitate   =>   **deep blue solution**

Paper 2 – Advanced Organic and Physical Chemistry (9CH0/02)

Topic 16 Kinetics II

Rate of Reaction

Definition of rate with equation

Rate depends on...

Rate Equation for general reaction with four points and a tip

Orders in respect to reactants (three points)

Overall order (two points)

Rate of Reaction (Speed)

Definition: Change of concentration (products or reactants) over time

$$r = \frac{\Delta c}{\Delta t}$$

r: rate of reaction $[\text{mol dm}^{-3}\text{ s}^{-1}]$
Δc: change of concentration
Δt: time interval

-> Rate depends on temperature; surface area; catalyst and **concentration of reactants** (pressure for gases) -> see Year 1 revision card "Rates of Reactions"

$$aA + bB \rightarrow cC + dD$$

Rate equation:

$$\text{rate} = k\,[A]^m\,[B]^n$$

k: rate constant
[ ]:   concentration
m: order with respect to reactant A
n: order with respect to reactant B

- Rate equation indicates how much the rate of the reaction depends on the concentrations of the reactants
- Can be used to calculate rate of reaction
- Products C, D do not appear in the rate equation because rate does not depend on product concentration, just reactants (collision theory: higher concentration -> collisions more likely)
- Catalyst (H^+) can appear in the rate equation (might not appear in reaction equation)
=> **rate equation has nothing to do with an equilibrium equation or the mole equation of the overall chemical reaction**

Orders m, n:
- 0 order in respect to A: rate of reaction does not depend on concentration of [A]: double [A] -> no change in rate of reaction
- 1st order in respect to A: double [A] -> rate doubles
- 2nd order in respect to A: double [A] -> rate quadruples
=> data table can be used to determine order in respect to reactant

Overall (total) order of reaction: m+n
- **Order of reaction indicates how many of reactant molecules are involved in the rate determining step (1st: one, 2nd: two molecules)**
- Order of reactant/reaction is determined empirically (experimentally): Concentration-Time graphs & Rate-Concentration graphs

---

Rate Constant k
&
Rate Determining Step

Properties of k (two points)

Applications

Units of k

Equation to calculate k

Example for unit calculation of 1st order reaction

Definition of rate-determining step

Relationship between moles of rate determining step and order

Two rules for rate determining step and reactants

Deduce rate determining step from rate equation with example

Rate constant k

- the larger k, the faster the reaction
- **k only temperature dependent**
  -> collision theory (kinetic energy > activation energy)
- applications: industry and enzymes
- units of k change depending on order

Calculate k and its units:

$$k = \frac{rate}{[A]^m[B]^n}$$

Example for unit calculation:

first order reaction: rate = k [A]

$$k = \frac{r}{[A]} = \frac{\cancel{mol\,dm^{-3}}\,s^{-1}}{\cancel{mol\,dm^{-3}}} = s^{-1}$$

Rate-Determining step

Definition: slowest step in a multistep reaction

I) Mole equation of the rate determining step indicates the order of the reactants in the rate equation and vice versa:

$1CH_3Cl + 1OH^- \rightarrow CH_3OH + Cl^-$ **slow (rate determining step)**

rate = $k[CH_3Cl]^1[HO^-]^1$

Rules:
- If a reactant is in the rate equation, it or a species derived from it, takes part in the rate-determining step.
- If a reactant is not in the rate equation, it or a species derived from it, **does not** take part in the rate-determining step.

II) Rate equation can be used to predict the rate-determining step

Example: Predict the rate-determining step of the **Iodform reaction**

$CH_3COCH_3 + I_2 \rightarrow CH_3COCH_2I + HI$ rate = $k[CH_3COCH_3][H^+]$

-> look up Iodoform reaction and Keto-Enol tautomerism for the full mechanism

S_N1 and S_N2 Mechanisms for Haloalkane Hydrolysis

These mechanisms can be concluded from....(two points).

Number of molecules involved in rate determining step of S_N1

Draw S_N1 mechanism

Optical activity of products

Molecule properties which favour this mechanism

(Conditions)

Number of molecules involved in rate determining step of S_N2

Draw S_N2 mechanism

Optical activity of products

Molecule properties which favour this mechanism

(Conditions)

S_N1 & S_N2 Mechanisms for Haloalkane Hydrolysis

These two mechanisms can be concluded from
- rate equations
- optical activity of the products

S_N1: Nucleophilic Substitution First Order

$$rate = k\ [RX]$$

=> **1** molecule (RX) involved in rate determining step -> *unimolecular*

Step 1:

Step 2:

Racemic mixture (two enantiomers)

-> **racemic mixture not optical active** -> see revision card 'Optical Isomers'

Carbocation stabilized by alkyl groups of RX: **tertiary best -> primary worst**

Conditions: weak base

S_N2: Nucleophilic Substitution Second Order

$$rate = k\ [RX][OH^-]$$

=> **2** molecules (RX & OH⁻) involved in rate determining step -> *bimolecular*

Transition state **One enantiomer** *(Inverted)*

-> **Single enantiomer** product is **optical active**   *(Walden Inversion)*

Attack from the rear: less alkyl groups -> more space => easier to attack C:
primary best -> tertiary worst

Conditions: strong base

Concentration-Time Graphs
&
Half-Life

Concentration-time graphs (three points & three graphs)

Methods to measure concentration-time graphs

(Maths – three points)

Definition of half-life

Half-life constant for...

Graph to determine half-life

Concentration-Time Graphs (Practical)

- to determine order in respect to reactant A by measuring [A] over time
- keep concentrations of other reactants, e.g. [B], constant by using **excess**
- shape of graph indicates order:

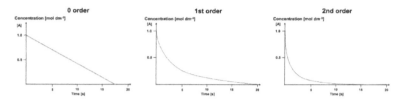

Concentration can be measured with different methods (see Year 1 revision card)
-> best if continuously measured (e.g. colorimeter -> absorption proportional to concentration)

Maths
- *Zero Order: constant gradient (= constant rate)*
- *For first order reactions: graph becomes a straight line if ln[A] is plotted against time (slope = -k)*
- *For second order reactions: graph becomes a straight line if 1/[A] is plotted against time (slope = k)*

Half-Life $t_{1/2}$

Definition: the time required to reach half the initial concentration

Half-life is constant for first order reactions:

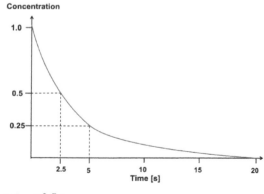

Concentration-time-graph: 1st order

-> $t_{1/2}$ = **2.5 s**

Rate-Concentration Graphs

How to create rate-concentration graphs (two points)

For 0 order reaction…

Initial rates method with graph (two points)

Rate-concentration graphs (three graphs and two points)

Iodine-clock

Rate-Concentration Graphs (Practical)

- To determine order with respect to reactant (A) by varying concentration of (A) and calculating initial rate of reactant from concentration-time graphs.
- Shape of graph indicates order.
- For 0 order reaction: gradient of concentration-time graph equals rate.

Initial rates method

- Measure time until set amount of product is formed and calculate rate   *or*
- Draw tangent through concentration at 0 s and calculate gradient to get initial rate for 1st and 2nd order reaction

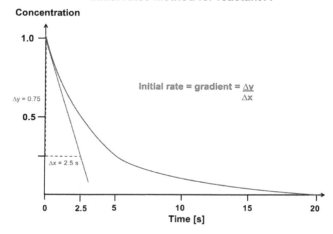

Initial rates method for reactant A

Plot **initial rates against concentration** of [A] to get rate-concentration graphs for A. Shape of graph indicates order:

Rate-Concentration Graphs

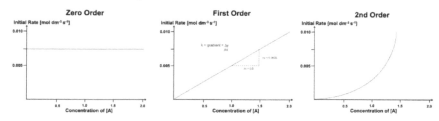

- For first order reactions: k = gradient of line
- For second order reactions: the graph becomes a straight line if plotted against $[A]^2$
- Iodine clock: Plot 1/t instead of rate to get same graphs -> much simpler

---

Iodine Clock

Purpose

Method

Relationship between time and rate (three points)

Two Applications

Iodine clock (Practical)

-> can be used to determine rate of reaction *(or activation energy E_a)*

Iodine is generated in a redox reaction **(slow reaction):**

> *1)* $2I^- + S_2O_8^{2-} \rightarrow I_2 + 2SO_4^{2-}$
> *(peroxidisulfate)*

> -> in the presence of starch a dark blue complex with I_2 would form,

but is removed immediately (fast reaction):

> *2)* $I_2 + 2S_2O_3^{2-} \rightarrow 2I^- + S_4O_6^{2-}$
> thiosulfate   *(tetrathionate)*

> -> colour does not appear until all of the thiosulfate $S_2O_3^{2-}$ is used up

The time (t) it takes until colour appears is inversely proportional to the rate (or rate constant k) of reaction
-> the faster the first reaction the shorter the time
-> this time t is measured with a stop watch and recorded
=> *reaction is like a* **stop watch** *(therefore called 'clock')*

If we change conditions (concentration/temperature) which increases the rate of the first reaction then the time until the colour appears shortens.

Applications

Rate-Concentration graphs
Plot 1/t instead of rate against concentration
-> measuring the time is much simpler than to determining rate
=> leads to the same graphs

Arrhenius Plot
Plot ln 1/t instead of ln k to determine activation energy E_a
-> measuring the time is much simpler than to determining rate constant k
* see revision card 'Arrhenius Equation'

Arrhenius Equation

Purpose

Arrhenius plot (four points)

Equation for gradient

Equation for E_a

Rule

Graph

Arrhenius Equation (Practical)

to calculate activation energy E_a

$$k = A \, e^{-Ea/RT} \qquad \text{-> data sheet}$$

k: rate constant
A: a constant
E_a: activation energy
R: gas constant $8.31 \, J \, K^{-1} \, mol^{-1} \, (N_A * k_B)$ -> *data sheet*
T: temperature in K

Arrhenius Plot
- vary temperature T and measure k (or t -> see "Iodine Clock")
- record in a table and plot ln k (or ln 1/t) against 1/T
- determine gradient m of line: $m = - E_a/R$
- rearrange equation towards $E_a = -(m \times R)$

$$ln \, k = - \frac{E_a}{R} \frac{1}{T} + lnA \qquad \text{-> logarithmic form of equation}$$

$$y \ = \ m * x \ + \ c \qquad \text{-> general equation for a linear graph}$$

plot ln k against 1/T to determine E_a **-> straight line (descending)**

gradient $-m = \dfrac{-E_a}{R}$ -> negative gradient (-m)

=> $E_a = -(-m \times 8.31) = m \times 8.31$

-> E_a is always positive

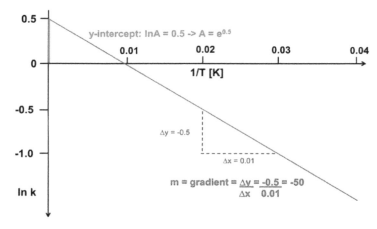

-> see also revision card 'Iodine Clock'

Topic 17 Organic Chemistry II

Optical Isomers

Definition of optical isomers

Definition of chiral centre

Two tips for chiral centre

Draw two optical isomers

Physical characteristics of optical isomers (two points)

Definition of racemic mixture with property

Applications (three points)

Optical Isomers

Definition

Optical Isomers (enantiomers) have a **chiral centre** and are
non-superimposable mirror images

Chiral centre

- **Definition: Four** different atoms/groups attached to one carbon atom
  -> **asymmetric carbon (*)**
- Look at the entire group not just the first Carbon atom of the sidechain to
  decide if they are different
- *Each chiral centre doubles the number of possible optical isomers of a
  molecule*

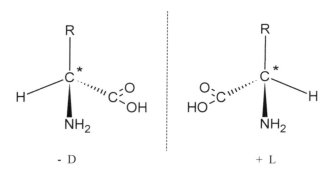

- D   + L

Physical characteristics

- they rotate polarised light anticlockwise (–) or clockwise (+)
  => **optically active**
- all other physical characteristics (melting points etc.) are the same

Racemic mixture (racemate)

- 50 : 50 mixture of both isomers (cancel each other out)
  => **not optically active**

Applications

- important for pharmaceutical drugs (thalidomide)
- amino acids
- enzymes: active sides and substrates

Aldehydes & Ketones

Naming

Properties of Carbonyl group

Mechanism of nucleophilic addition with $LiAlH_4$

Reaction equation for reduction of aldehyde

Mechanism of nucleophilic addition with HCN (two points)

Six tests for aldehydes/ketones

Aldehydes/Ketones

$$H_3C-\overset{\overset{\displaystyle O\,\delta-}{\|}}{\underset{}{C}}{}^{\delta+}-CH_3$$

Propanone (propan-2-one)

$$H_3C-CH_2-C\overset{O\;\delta-}{\underset{H}{\diagup}}{}^{\delta+}$$

Propanal

Carbonyl group   C=O
Permanent Dipole $\delta+$ $\delta-$, **but not a good leaving group (double bond)**

Nucleophilic addition / Reduction with LiAlH$_4$ lithium aluminiumhydride

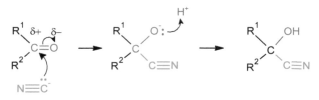

hydride (nucleophile)   secondary alcohol
$(CH_3)_2CO + 2[H] \rightarrow (CH_3)_2CHOH$ [H]: reducing unit (donating 1e$^-$)

Nucleophilic addition with HCN (hydrogen cyanide) to form hydroxynitriles

cyanide (nucleophile, toxic!)   hydroxynitrile

-> CN$^-$ can attack planar carbonyl group from both sides -> **racemate**
-> KCN/H$_2$SO$_4$ preferred to HCN (weak acid), because of larger amount of CN$^-$

Tests to distinguish between Aldehydes and Ketones (Practical)

Tollens: test for aldehydes (AgNO$_3$/ammonia, test tube in warm water bath)
      $2Ag^+ + Aldehyde_{(+1)} \rightarrow$ Carboxylic acid$_{(+3)}$ + **2Ag** (silver **mirror)**
      -> aldehyde is oxidised, silver ions reduced

Fehling: test for aldehydes (gentle heating, Cu^{2+}/NaOH/*tartaric acid*)
$2Cu^{2+}_{blue} + Aldehyde \rightarrow 2Cu^+ +$ Carboxylic acid (Cu$_2$O precipitate - brick red)
Benedict's reagent: Same as Fehling but Na$_2$CO$_3$ instead of NaOH

Acidified potassium dichromate -> see Year 1 revision card 'Alcohols'

Brady's reagent: 2,4-DNPH -> **test for carbonyl group**
      -> orange **precipitate** => **different melting points** for aldehyde/ketone

Iodoform reaction (Iodine & NaOH) -> yellow precipitate for **methyl carbonyl**

Carboxylic Acids

Naming of carboxylic acids in homologous series

Name and properties and of the functional group

Characteristics of carboxylic acids (six points)

Acid-base reaction with equation

Three tests for carboxylic acids

Two methods of preparation

Four organic reactions

Carboxylic Acids

Homologous Series: Methanoic acid , ethanoic acid, propanoic acid,...

Carboxyl group: strong dipole -> more polar than alcohols or aldehydes/ketones
=> OH good leaving group: **nucleophilic addition-elimination reactions**

Characteristics

- High boiling points due to Hydrogen-bonds (Dimers)
- Aldehyde/ketones have no H-bonds, but form them with water -> soluble
- Boiling points increase with chain length (London forces)
- Solubility in water decreases with chain length *(more hydrophobic)*
- **IR: broad absorption band of OH group at** *2500-3300 cm^{-1}* and
  sharp peak of CO group at *1620-1820 cm^{-1} (data sheet)*
- **they are weak acids:**

Acid-base reaction

$2CH_3COOH + CuO$ (base) -> $(CH_3COO)_2Cu + H_2O$
salt – copper(II) ethano**ate**

Tests (Practical)

	colour change
pH-Indicator	
R-COOH + **carbonate** -> salt + water + $CO_{2(g)}$	fizzing**, carbonate disappears**
R-COOH + metal -> salt (carboxylate) + $H_{2(g)}$	fizzing**, metal disappears**

Preparation

- Oxidation of primary alcohols or aldehydes
- Hydrolysis of Nitriles R-CN (dilute HCl, reflux, then distillation)
  R-CN + 2H$_2$O + HCl -> R-COOH + NH$_4$Cl

Organic Reactions

- They form **Esters** with alcohols (see revision card 'Esters')
- They are **reduced** to primary alcohols by **LiAlH$_4$ in dry ether**
  R-COOH + 4[H] -> R-CH$_2$OH + H$_2$O
- **Preparation of Acylchloride:**
  R-COOH + PCl$_5$ -> R-COCl + POCl$_3$ + HCl
- They **cannot be oxidised** except methanoic acid due to its aldehyde group:
  HCOOH + [O] -> H$_2$CO$_3$ (decomposes: $H_2O + CO_2$ => fizzing)

Esters

Equation for esterification reaction

Naming of esters

Conditions, properties and types of reaction (four points)

Polyesters

Physical characteristics of esters (five points)

Applications (three points)

IR

Two methods of ester hydrolysis

Fats/oils

Esters

Esterification

$$H_3C-\overset{\displaystyle O}{\underset{\displaystyle OH}{C}} \quad + \quad HO-CH_3 \quad \underset{}{\overset{H_2SO_4 \text{ conc}}{\rightleftharpoons}} \quad H_3C-\overset{\displaystyle O}{\underset{\displaystyle O-CH_3}{C}} \quad + \quad H_2O$$

| carboxylic acid | + | alcohol | $\rightleftharpoons$ | Ester | + | water |
| ethanoic acid | + | methanol | | methyl ethanoate | | |

- **Conditions:** Reflux, catalyst: concentrated sulfuric acid
- Reversible reaction, equilibrium (low yield)
- **Condensation, Nucleophilic Addition-Elimination reaction**
- *Substitution of H of carboxylic acid with -R from alcohol*

Polyester
-> see revision card 'Condensation Polymers'

Physical characteristics of esters
- Nice smell
- Neutral (no acid reactions)
- Low boiling point (no hydrogen bonds)
- They are functional group isomers of carboxylic acids
- Less polar than carboxylic acids

Applications
- Perfumes & flavouring (peach, pineapple, raspberry)
- Biodiesel (methyl esters of long-chain carboxylic acids)
- Solvents & plasticisers

IR
Esters do not show the broad absorption band of carboxylic acids at *2500 – 3000 cm^{-1}* (OH-group)

Ester hydrolysis

hot diluted H_2SO_4 or HCl:
$$CH_3COOCH_3 + H_2O \rightleftharpoons CH_3COOH + CH_3OH$$
carboxylic acid

hot aqueous NaOH: $CH_3COOCH_3 + NaOH \rightarrow CH_3COONa + CH_3OH$
sodium carboxylate
-> **soap** (salts of long-chain carboxylic acids from fats)

Fats/Oils
Natural esters of propane-1,2,3-triol (glycerol) with fatty acids

Acyl Chlorides

Structural Formula

Characteristics of acyl group (three points)

Four acylation reactions with equations

Warning

Numbering of carbon atoms

Preparation of acylchloride with equation

Acylchlorides

$$H_3C - C \underset{Cl\ \delta-}{\overset{O\ \delta-}{\big|}} \delta+$$

Ethanoyl chloride

Acyl-group: highly reactive C (high $\delta+$ charge -> strongly attracts nucleophiles)
=> **nucleophilic substitution (addition-elimination) reactions**
=> Cl good leaving group; gets substituted

Acylation reactions

$RCOCl + H_2O \quad \rightarrow \quad R-C\overset{O}{\underset{OH}{}} \quad + HCl \qquad$ **Carboxylic acid**

$R^1COCl + CH_3OH \quad \rightarrow \quad R^1-C\overset{O}{\underset{O-R^2}{}} \quad + HCl \qquad$ **Ester (R^2: CH_3); white fumes**

$RCOCl + NH_{3conc} \quad \rightarrow \quad R-C\overset{O}{\underset{NH_2}{}} \quad + HCl \qquad$ **Primary Amide**

$R^1COCl + CH_3NH_2 \quad \rightarrow \quad R^1-C\overset{O}{\underset{NH-R^2}{}} \quad + HCl \qquad$ **Sec. Amide (R^2: CH_3)**

Caution: vigorous reactions; very acidic and corrosive HCl produced

Numbering of Carbon atoms
- Starts with the carbon of the acyl-group => 1 (similar to carboxylic acids)

Preparation of Acylchloride
$$R\text{-}COOH + PCl_5 \rightarrow R\text{-}COCl + POCl_3 + HCl$$

Topic 18 Organic Chemistry III

Benzene & Arenes

Characteristics of benzene (three points)

Draw p-orbitals and electron clouds (two drawings)

Evidence for delocalised structure (three points)

Naming (two points)

Test for benzene

Reaction type of arenes with reason

Draw mechanism

Tip

Electron donating groups

Electron withdrawing groups

Benzene

Characteristics
- p-orbitals of π-bonds overlap
- π-electrons **delocalised** (symbolised by the ring in the structural formula; cannot polarise halogens like alkenes do)
- **high electron densities** (electron clouds) above and below carbon ring

Evidence for delocalised structure
- C-C-bonds have same length (Kekulé: different lengths for single and double bonds) -> planar ring
- *does not decolourise bromine water*
- hydrogenation enthalpy less exothermic than compared to 3 x cyclohexene

Naming
- 1-chloro-4-methylbenzene (alphabetic, smallest number)
- Name if side group: Phenyl C_6H_5- *(not Benzyl $C_6H_5CH_2$-)*

Test: burns with smoky flame (soot)

Arenes – aromatic compounds

Reactions: electrophilic substitutions (E$^+$: Electrophile)
    -> to keep delocalised system (low energy) *(Alkenes – Addition)*

Benzene   +   E$^+$ ->   E-benzene   +   H$^+$

-> First curly arrow must touch or cross the inside ring

Electron donating groups: -OH, -NH$_2$
Lone pair of e$^-$ is delocalized into the ring and increases the electron density
=> directs substituents to **carbons 2, 4 & 6**

Electron withdrawing groups: -NO$_2$, -COOH
Higher electronegativity of nitrogen withdraws electrons from the ring and decreases the electron density => directs substituents to **carbons 3 & 5**

Reactions of Arenes

Nitration with three equations and conditions (three points)

Halogenation with three equations

Alkylation with two equations and conditions

Acylation reaction with two equations and conditions

Combustion with oxygen

Reactions of Arenes

-> Electrophilic Substitutions

Nitration with nitric acid

$H_2SO_4 + HNO_3 \rightarrow HSO_4^- + NO_2^+ + H_2O$ nitronium ion -> E^+ ($^+$ on N)

$H^+ + HSO_4^- \rightarrow H_2SO_4$ -> regeneration of catalyst with H^+ from benzene

$C_6H_6 \quad + \quad HNO_3 \quad \rightarrow \quad C_6H_5NO_2 \quad + \quad H_2O$
                         nitrobenzene

-> Concentrated HNO_3, sulphuric acid catalyst, below 55 °C (mononitration).
Above 55 °C -> multiple nitrations
-> Reduction of nitrobenzene to aminobenzene for dyes

Halogenations (Chlorination/Bromination)

Halogen carriers: AlCl$_3$ (AlBr$_3$) or **FeCl$_3$** (FeX$_3$) or **Fe** needed as a catalyst to form X^+ ions (polarise halogen).

$AlCl_3 + Cl_2 \rightarrow AlCl_4^-$ (dative) $+ Cl^+$ (E^+)   heterolytic fission; dative bond
$AlCl_4^- + H^+ \rightarrow AlCl_3 + HCl$ **-> regeneration of catalyst**

$C_6H_6 \quad + \quad Cl_2 \quad \rightarrow \quad C_6H_5Cl \quad + \quad HCl$
                      1-chlorobenzene (phenylchloride)
   -> same reaction with Br_2 instead of Cl_2

Alkylation (Friedel Crafts)

$CH_3CH_2Cl + AlCl_3 \rightarrow CH_3CH_2^+ + AlCl_4^-$ R^+ -> alkyl ($^+$ on C)
$C_6H_6 \quad + \quad CH_3CH_2^+ \quad \rightarrow \quad C_6H_5CH_2CH_3 \quad + \quad H^+$ (ethylbenzene)
benzene $\quad + \quad R^+ \quad \rightarrow \quad$ benzene-R   (alkylbenzene)
-> anhydrous $AlCl_3$, heat under reflux

Acylation (Friedel Crafts) with acylchoride (anhydrous AlCl$_3$, heat, reflux)

$AlCl_4^- + H^+ \rightarrow AlCl_3 + HCl$ -> regeneration of catalyst

                          Phenylketone
$C_6H_6 \quad + \quad RCOCl \quad \rightarrow \quad C_6H_5COR \quad + \quad HCl$

Combustion with oxygen

       $2C_6H_6 \quad + \quad 15O_2 \quad \rightarrow \quad 12CO_2 \quad + \quad 6H_2O$
       -> smoky flame (incomplete combustion => C, soot)

Phenol

Five characteristics

Electrophilic Substitution Reactions (five points)

Equation for halogenation reaction (three points)

Esterification reaction (one point)

Synthesis of Aspirin with equation and preparation steps

Four applications

Phenol

Characteristics
- High boiling point (Hydrogen-bonds)
- Very weak acid but very corrosive
- **Acid reactions** (see revision card 'carboxylic acids'):
  $NaOH + C_6H_5OH \rightarrow C_6H_5O^-Na^+ + H_2O$ (sodium phenoxide/phenolate)
  $Na + C_6H_5OH \rightarrow C_6H_5O^-Na^+ + \frac{1}{2}H_2$ (fizzing) -> test for phenol
- **but no fizzing with carbonates** *or hydrogen carbonates* -> too weak
- Numbering of carbons starts with the carbon connected to OH => 1

Electrophilic Substitution Reactions
- More reactive than other arenes:
- Lone pairs of electrons of the oxygen atom are **delocalised** into the ring and activate **2, 6** *(ortho)* and **4** *(para)* positions for electrophiles, by **increasing electron density** (can polarise halogens)
- Directs electrophiles to these positions -> rev. card 'Benzene & Arenes'
- **No catalyst required for halogenation (halogen is polarised)**
- *Nitration with diluted instead of concentrated HNO_3 (no H_2SO_4 catalyst required) => 2-nitrophenol*

Halogenation (Practical):

2,4,6-tribromophenol

- **Bromine water decolourises spontaneously** (orange -> colourless)
- Three bromine atoms bound to the ring instead of just one with benzene
- Product is a white solid

Esterification with acid anhydrides or acyl chlorides

$CH_3COCl + C_6H_5OH \rightarrow CH_3COOC_6H_5 + HCl$

- Anhydrides are safer and cheaper than acyl chlorides

Synthesis of Aspirin from salicylic acid (Practical)

salicylic acid + ethanoic anhydride -> acetylsalicylic acid + ethanoic acid

- Warm the reaction mixture, cool, filter aspirin crystals and recrystallise

Applications: Plastics; resin in paints; antiseptics; disinfectants

Amines

Four types of amines

Naming

Four types of reactions of amines including cause

Mechanism of reaction with haloalkane

Amines

primary R-NH$_2$, secondary R$_2$NH, tertiary R$_3$N, quaternary R$_4$N$^+$

ammonium salt

Naming

CH$_3$CH$_2$NH$_2$: 1-Ethylamine, 1-aminoethan   -> aliphatic amine

C$_6$H$_5$-NH$_2$:   phenylamine (aminobenzene)   -> aromatic amine

Lone pair of electrons on nitrogen causes reactions as:

I) Bases

CH$_3$CH$_2$NH$_2$ + HCl -> CH$_3$CH$_2$NH$_3$Cl   (CH$_3$CH$_2$NH$_3$$^+$ + Cl$^-$)

Ethylamine   ethylammonium chloride (salt)

Aliphatic amine -> stronger bases than ammonia *(Inductive Effect)*

Aromatic amine -> weaker bases (lone pair delocalises into the ring)

II) Alkalis (weak): CH$_3$CH$_2$NH$_2$ + H$_2$O -> CH$_3$CH$_2$NH$_3$$^+$ + **OH$^-$**

III) Ligands

Ligand exchange reaction with [Cu(H$_2$O)$_6$]$^{2+}$

-> see revision card 'Complexes'

IV) Nucleophiles

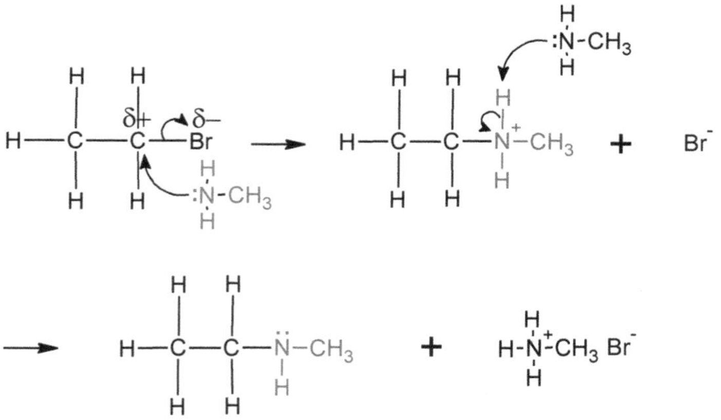

bromoalkane + **prim amine** -> **sec amine** + alkylammonium bromide

-> **nucleophilic substitution** *(second attack of amine as base)*

-> see also Year 1 revision card 'Haloalkanes'

Preparation of Amines & Amides

Preparation of aliphatic amines with equation and conditions

Products with excess RX

Aliphatic amines from nitriles with equation and conditions

Naming nitriles

Preparation of aromatic amines (equations & conditions)

Preparation of amides with equation

Test for amines

Naming amides

Preparation of Amines

Aliphatic Amines from haloalkanes (Nucleophilic Substitution)

$$R\text{-}X + 2NH_3 \rightarrow R\text{-}NH_2 + NH_4X$$

Conditions: heat in a sealed flask with excess ammonia in ethanol

With excess RX:

continues to substitute H with R until R_4N^+ (quaternary ammonium) formed
=> **mixture** of primary, secondary, tertiary and quaternary amines
-> this mixture can be separated by **fractional distillation**

Quaternary ammonium salts used as cationic surfactants (detergent, emulsifier)

Aliphatic Amines from Nitriles (Reduction)

$$R\text{-}CN + 4[H] \rightarrow R\text{-}CH_2NH_2$$
nitrile   amine

Conditions:

- Ni/H_2, high temperature & pressure (catalytic hydrogenation)   *or*
- $LiAlH_4$ in dry ether (expensive, lab)

-> for preparation of nitriles see Year 1 revision card 'Haloalkanes'

Naming Nitriles: $CH_3CH(CH_3)CH_2CN$ 3-Methylbutanenitrile

Aromatic Amines from Nitro compounds (Reduction)

$$C_6H_5NO_2 + 6[H] \rightarrow C_6H_5NH_2 + 2H_2O$$

-> Reflux, Sn/HCl_{conc} => **Reduction** with H_2, then $NaOH_{(aq)}$
-> **phenylamine** is used for formation of **Azo dyes**

Preparation of Amides

From Acylchlorides

$$RCOCl + NH_3 \rightarrow RCONH_2 + HCl \,(NH_4Cl) \qquad \text{Primary Amide}$$

=> See revision card 'Acyl Chlorides'
=> **Test for Amines:** white fumes of **HCl** turn litmus paper from blue to red

Naming Amides:

N-methylethanamide

Condensation Polymers

Condensation polymerization (two points)

Polyamide preparation with two equations

Circling method

Polyester preparation with two equations

Definition of diol

Drawing lines method

Both functional groups on same molecule

How to recognise an addition polymer

Condensation Polymers

Condensation polymerization
- **Monomers form a polymer and another small molecule (H_2O)**
- Monomers must have two functional groups

I) Polyamide

dicarboxylic acid + diamine   ->   poly-amide + water

Propane-1,3-dicarboxylic acid + 1,2 diamino-ethane

=> Circle **atoms which form the** water. **The leftover** half-bonds **form the** amide bonds

II) Polyester

dicarboxylic (dioic) acid + diol   ->   poly-ester + water

Propane-1,3-dicarboxylic (dioic) acid + ethan-1,2-diol

Diol: compound with two alcohol (-OH) groups

To determine monomers from a chain:
draw lines through the middle of the ester bonds and add water (OH, H) to CO and O respectively (hydrolysis)

Carboxylic acid and alcohol group on same molecule -> poly-ester + water

-> *acyl chlorides can be used instead of carboxylic acids*

If the polymer chain (repeat unit) is not connected by amide or ester groups, but C-C single bonds, then it is an addition polymer

-> See also Year 1 revision card 'Addition Polymers'

Amino Acids & Proteins

Definition of amino acids

Optical isomers

Definition of amphoteric

Draw structural formulae at three different pH

Definition of zwitterion

Building blocks of...

Ester formation

Peptide formation with equation and reaction type

Circling method

Two methods of peptide hydrolysis with equations

Amino acids

Def.: alpha-amino-carboxylic acids (NH_2 and COOH attached to same carbon *)

Optical isomers: chiral centre * -> 4 different groups at alpha C (except glycine)

Amphoteric: react as acid & base *(bifunctional molecule)* -> weak buffer

acidic (*protonated*)   intermediate pH (**zwitterion**)   alkaline (*deprotonated*)

Zwitterion: has positive and negative charges at intermediate pH
-> ionic bonds, high melting points (stronger than H-bonds) => solid salts

Building blocks of Proteins: Proteins are polypeptides -> **enzymes (biological catalysts)**

Carboxylic acid group: Ester-formation (cyclic ester with internal OH-group)
                -> see revision card 'Esters'

Peptide Formation (Dimer)

Alanine   Glycine   Dipeptide (AlaGly)   +   water
-> Condensation

=> Circle **atoms which form the** water, **then connect the leftover** half-bonds
to form a peptide bond (amide)

-> **you could also get dipeptide GlyAla**

Peptide Hydrolysis

With acid:
6 M HCl, reflux heat; then neutralize
Peptide + H_2O (H^+) => protonated amino acids (+)

With alkaline:
$NaOH_{conc}$
Peptide + OH^- => deprotonated amino acids (-) (carboxylate-salt)

Preparation and Purification of Organic Compounds

Apparatus used for preparation (two points)

Five purification methods:

Washing (two points)

Drying (one point)

Recrystallisation including method (five points)

Distillation (two points)

Solvent extraction

Tests for purity (three points)

Preparation: Reflux apparatus
- To heat a reaction mixture safely
- Electrical heaters (heating mantel) are used to avoid naked flames which could ignite flammable organic compounds
-> See Year 1 revision card 'Reflux Apparatus' for details

Purification
The products of a reaction are often contaminated with side-products or unreacted reactants. The following methods are applied to remove these:

I) Washing
- A solid product can be washed with water or an organic solvent by filtration under reduced pressure (**Büchner flask**)
- Acids can be removed by reaction with $NaHCO_3$. Water and CO_2 are formed. The water insoluble organic product can be separated by using a **separating funnel** (see Year 1 revision card 'Separating Funnel')

II) Drying
- Traces of water can be removed from a liquid by adding anhydrous salts (CaCl2, MgSO4) -> See Year 1 revision card 'Drying with Anhydrous Salts'

III) Recrystallisation
-> Removes small amounts of impurities from a solid compound, which is very soluble at high temperatures and insoluble at low temperatures
- Hot solvent is added to the impure solid until it just dissolves -> saturated
- Hot filtration to remove insoluble impurities
- The solution is slowly cooled down until crystals of the product are formed
- The impurities remain in the solution, due to their lower concentrations
- The pure product crystals are filtered, washed with cold solvent and dried
-> See Year 1 revision card 'Recrystallisation'

IV) Distillation
- The liquid product can be separated from impurities according to their different boiling points
- **Steam distillation:** steam is added to reduce the boiling point of the product, to prevent decomposition at high temperatures
-> See Year 1 revision card 'Distillation Apparatus'

V) Solvent extraction: See Year 1 revision card 'Separating Funnel'

Tests for Purity
- A pure substance has a specific melting and boiling point, which can be compared to literature values. **Impurities lower melting point** and **increase boiling point** -> larger range.
- **Measuring the melting point:** the solid is slowly heated in a capillary tube, in a beaker of oil containing a thermometer; the temperature is read when the solid melts.
- **Measuring the boiling point:** use a distillation apparatus.

Extending Carbon Chain Length

Introduction

Preparation of Grignard reagent with equation and condition

Three Grignard reactions involving two steps

Two methods for nitrile formations

Two nitrile reactions with equations

Formation of C-C bonds in arenes

Extending Carbon Chain Length

-> C-C bonds are difficult to make

Reactions to extend a carbon chain for aliphatic compounds:

Preparation of Grignard Reagent in dry ether

CH_3CH_2I + Mg -> CH_3CH_2MgI
haloalkane   Ethyl magnesium iodide
The alkyl rest of the Grignard reagent has a negative charge -> Nucleophile R^-

Grignard Reactions

Two Steps: 1.) Grignard & carbon compound in dry ether; 2.) diluted HCl

With Aldehydes

R^1MgI + $R^2-C\overset{O}{\underset{H}{}}$ + HCl -> $R^2-\overset{OH}{\underset{H}{C}}-R^1$ + $MgICl$

Secondary alcohol (primary R^2=H)

With Ketones

R^1MgI + $R^1-C\overset{O}{\underset{R^2}{}}$ + HCl -> $R^2-\overset{OH}{\underset{R^3}{C}}-R^1$ + $MgICl$

Tertiary alcohol

With CO_2

R^1MgI + CO_2 + HCl -> R^1COOH + $MgICl$

Carboxylic acid

Nitrile Formation

I) Nucleophilic Substitution of haloalkanes with cyanide

R-X + KCN -> R-CN + KX   (nitrile + potassium halide)
-> for mechanism see Year 1 revision card 'Haloalkanes'

II) Nucleophilic addition reaction of carbonyl compounds with HCN (toxic!)

R^1COR^2 + HCN -> $R^1COH(CN)R^2$
hydrogen cyanide   hydroxynitrile
-> see revision cards 'Aldehydes & Ketones' and 'Carboxylic Acids'

Formation of C-C bond in Arenes

-> see Friedel-Crafts reactions on revision card 'Reactions of Arenes'

Topic 19 Modern Analytical Techniques II

NMR Spectroscopy: H-NMR & Carbon 13-NMR

Method

Y- and x-axis of NMR spectrum

Four characteristics of H-NMR spectrum

Solvent

Converting ppm into %

Three reasons for use of TMS

Two Applications

Carbon 13-NMR (three points)

NMR spectroscopy

Method: Radio waves of a specific frequency (resonance frequency) are absorbed by the nucleus of an atom. This reverses the spin of the nucleus inside a **strong magnetic field.** (Nucleus must have odd number of nucleons)

Proton H-NMR (nuclear magnetic resonance)

NMR spectrum
Absorption (y) of electromagnetic waves against chemical shift δ (x)
-> gives information about number and position of H-atoms in a molecule:

- **Number of peaks:** number of **different H environments (types)**
- **Position of peak:** **functional group** (different shielding)
  Chemical shift δ: resonance frequency of functional group in **ppm** relative to **TMS** (internal standard, tetramethylsilane $Si(CH_3)_4$)
  ppm: parts per million -> a percentage
- **Number above peak: number of protons (H)** of same type
  -> from **integration ratio / relative peak area / relative intensity / integration trace (use ruler)**
- **Spin-spin coupling:** main peak splits off into smaller peaks **(n+1)**
  -> doublet, triplet, quartet etc. => **Splitting pattern**
  -> indicates **number of neighbouring H: n**
  -> **H have to be bound to adjacent Carbons**
  -> H bounded to other elements do not split: OH, NH
  -> only visible in high resolution NMR

Solvent: $CDCl_3$ *(deuterated chloroform)* or **CCl_4** (H free to prevent interference)

Converting ppm into percentage: $\qquad \% = \dfrac{ppm}{10,000}$

Reasons for use of TMS
- gives just one, strong signal away from others
- non-toxic and inert
- low boiling point -> easy to remove from sample

Applications

MRS/MRI: Magnetic resonance scanning/imaging with low energy electromagnetic waves (radio waves) in medicine
Chemistry: helps to determine the structure of an unknown compound

Carbon 13–NMR

- number of peaks indicates number of different carbon environments
- chemical shift -> chemical environment of carbon => **functional group**
- for arenes look at line of symmetry

How to predict NMR Spectrum from Structural Formula

Five Steps

Example butanone

Two common peaks with peak areas and splitting patterns

How to predict H-NMR spectrum from structural formula

- Circle the same types of hydrogens in the structural formula to get the number of peaks
- Count the number of hydrogens inside the circle. This is the number of hydrogens for that peak (peak area) => write number on top of the circle
- Count how many hydrogens are attached to adjacent carbons (n) to get the splitting pattern (n+1 -> doublet, triplet etc.) => write on top of the circle
- Identify the functional group the hydrogens belong to and get chemical shift from the table *(data sheet)* => write below the circle
- Compare this data to actual H-NMR spectra given

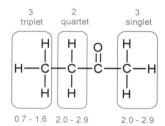

=> three peaks: 3H triplet   at 1.0 ppm,
                  2H quartet   at 2.5 ppm
                  3H singlet   at 2.3 ppm

Common peaks

A) One peak with peak area 6 ($\delta = 0.8 - 2.0$)   *isopropyl*

Splitting pattern: doublet

B) Two peaks with peak areas 2 and 3 ($\delta = 0.8 - 2.0$)   **ethyl**

Splitting patterns: 2 -> quartet, quintet or sextet; 3 -> triplet

---

Thin Layer Chromatography
&
Mass Spectroscopy

Purpose of chromatography

Two causes of separation

Application

TLC steps:

Stationary and mobile phase

Method (seven points)

How to treat colourless compounds (three methods)

Biochemical application

Equation for R_f value

High Resolution Mass spectroscopy

Application and Method (two points)

Tip

Chromatography

-> Separating and identifying components of a mixture (**solutes**) by degree of interaction with the stationary phase:

- Separation due to different **adsorption** to **solid** matrix -> **TLC, GC**
- or different **solubility (liquid)** -> **GLC**

Application: Quality control in industry (purity & identity)

TLC Thin Layer Chromatography (Practical)

- **Stationary phase (solid matrix):** silica (SiO_2) or alumina (Al_2O_3) coated glass/plastic plate
- **Mobile phase:** liquid solvent (alcohol, ester)
- Spots of the mixture and reference substances are put on a pencil line at the lower edge of the plate (starting point)
- The plate is placed in a beaker with liquid below the pencil line
- Liquid travels up the plate by capillary forces taking the compounds with it
- The components travel at different speeds due to different adsorption
- The plate is taken out when sufficient separation is achieved (**end point**)
- Mark the position of the solvent front with a pencil
- Compare R_f value of the unknown component with that of the known/pure compound (reference)
- Colourless compounds (**amino acids**) have to be treated with **ninhydrin, iodine** or **UV light** to make them visible on the dried plate
- Standard method **to separate and identify amino acids** after **hydrolysis** of **proteins**

R_f value:

$$R_f = \frac{a}{x}$$

a: distance moved by solute (compound) in cm
x: distance moved by solvent in cm
R_f: **Retardation Factor (retention factor)**

Mass Spectroscopy

-> see **Year1 revision card 'Mass Spectrometry'**

High-Resolution Mass Spectrometry

- Accurate Isotopic masses can be used to distinguish between compounds
- M_r of different compounds will vary by decimal places,
  e.g. compound with $M_r = 43.9898$ is CO_2 not C_3H_8 (44.0624)
  Relative isotopic masses: H = 1.0078, C = 12.0000, O = 15.9949
- **Do not use Relative atomic mass from periodic table for isotopic mass**

Gas Chromatography
&
HPLC

Three parts of the GLC Apparatus

Chromatogram (two points)

Definition and application of retention time

Method of identifying the component

Limitations (three points)

GC-MS

Applications (two points)

HPLC:

Two applications

Stationary and mobile phase

Method (five points)

Gas Chromatography (GC) and Gas Liquid Chromatography (GLC)

Apparatus
- **Inlet:** injection of liquid (heated to vaporize) or gas sample (not heated)
- **Column:**
  - filled with viscous liquid (GLC) or solid (GC) stationary phase
  - stream of unreactive carrier gas (N_2, He) as mobile phase
  - temperature is kept constant
- **Detector**

Chromatogram
- Absorption versus time
- *Area under peak gives percentage of individual component in the mixture*

Retention time
Definition: The time from injection of the sample to the component leaving the column

-> Identify the component by comparing retention time with that of the pure substance (reference) => if identical then it is confirmed

Limitations
- Unknown compounds might not have reference retention times
- Different components might have the same retention times
- Substances with high boiling points cannot be separated

GC-MS: An unknown compound leaving Gas Chromatography (GC) is identified by its fragmentation pattern in Mass Spectrometry (MS)

Applications
- Drug and alcohol level in blood (forensics)
- Airport security

HPLC (High Performance/Pressure Liquid Chromotography)
- For purifying an organic product or identifying components of a mixture
- **Stationary phase:** silica (SiO_2) bonded to hydrocarbons in steel tube
- **Mobile phase:** liquid solvent, e.g. polar mixture of methanol and water
- The sample mixture is run through the column and the time for each component to leave the column **(retention time)** is recorded
- High pressure is applied to reduce separation time
- Components separate according to solubility
- Retention time is compared to database to identify components
- Mass Spectrometry is combined with HPLC to better identify substances

Tips for Organic Synthesis
&
Tests for Functional Groups
&
Tips for Combined Techniques Questions

What to do with the structural formula (four points)

If the product is given...

If the reactant is given...

Tests for seven functional groups:

alkenes, haloalkanes, carbonyls, aldehydes,

alcohols, carboxylic acids, phenols

Four tips for combined technique questions

Tips for Organic Synthesis Questions

- Circle and label the functional groups in the structural formula
- The main functional group is most likely involved in the synthesis
- Recall the revision cards for each functional group remembering their characteristics, favourite reaction types, reactants, products and conditions
- Deduce from the information given (reactants, products, conditions) what is the most likely reaction to happen
- If the product is given, draw lines through the molecule, especially next to side chains or functional groups, to identify fragments which could give clues to the reactants *(synthons for retrosynthesis)*
- If the reactant is given, go through all possible reactions of the different functional groups from the revision card, and choose the most suitable one according to the product or conditions given.
  Example: 4-aminophenol is the reactant
  - The amino group could react as a base (neutralization) or a nucleophile (nucleophilic substitution)
  - The phenol group could react as an acid (neutralization) or an alcohol (esterification)
  - The phenol ring could act as an arene (electrophilic substitution)
- Memorise diagrams of organic synthetic routes (aliphatic, aromatic, alcohols etc.) from revision guides, to familiarise yourself with the different reaction routes and conditions

Tests for Functional Groups (Practical)

Alkenes: decolourisation of bromine -> Y1 revision card 'Alkenes'
Haloalkanes: precipitation reaction with silver nitrate -> Y1 revision card
Carbonyl compounds: orange precipitate with 2.4-DNPH -> Y2 revision card
Aldehydes: silver mirror with Tollens' reagent -> Y2 revision card
Alcohols: colour change of acidified $K_2Cr_2O_7$ (orange/green) -> Y1 revision card
Carboxylic acids: fizzing with carbonates -> Y2 revision card
Phenols: fizzing with alkali metals but not with carbonates -> Y2 revision card

Tips for Combined Techniques Questions

- First try to get the molecular formula from the elemental analysis data (-> empirical formula) and the molecular ion peak of the mass spectrum (see Year 1 revision cards). (To get the number of carbons, subtract the M_r of the functional group from the Mr of the whole molecule and divide by 12).
- Identify functional groups through the information given (test tube reactions -> see above) and IR spectrum (or chemical shifts of H- and C-13 NMR).
- Draw all possible isomers according to the molecular formula and check which structure fits the NMR spectra
- Even if you do not find a structure, describe and characterise all peaks of the spectra according to the data table. This ensures you will still get marks.

The Periodic Table of Elements

(1)	(2)		(3)	(4)	(5)	(6)	(7)	(8)	(9)	(10)	(11)	(12)	(13)	(14)	(15)	(16)	(17)	0 (8)
1	2		3	4	5	6	7						(13)	(14)	(15)	(16)	7	(18)
								1.0 H hydrogen 1										4.0 He helium 2
6.9 Li lithium 3	9.0 Be beryllium 4												10.8 B boron 5	12.0 C carbon 6	14.0 N nitrogen 7	16.0 O oxygen 8	19.0 F fluorine 9	20.2 Ne neon 10
23.0 Na sodium 11	24.3 Mg magnesium 12												27.0 Al aluminium 13	28.1 Si silicon 14	31.0 P phosphorus 15	32.1 S sulfur 16	35.5 Cl chlorine 17	39.9 Ar argon 18
39.1 K potassium 19	40.1 Ca calcium 20		45.0 Sc scandium 21	47.9 Ti titanium 22	50.9 V vanadium 23	52.0 Cr chromium 24	54.9 Mn manganese 25	55.8 Fe iron 26	58.9 Co cobalt 27	58.7 Ni nickel 28	63.5 Cu copper 29	65.4 Zn zinc 30	69.7 Ga gallium 31	72.6 Ge germanium 32	74.9 As arsenic 33	79.0 Se selenium 34	79.9 Br bromine 35	83.8 Kr krypton 36
85.5 Rb rubidium 37	87.6 Sr strontium 38		88.9 Y yttrium 39	91.2 Zr zirconium 40	92.9 Nb niobium 41	95.9 Mo molybdenum 42	[98] Tc technetium 43	101.1 Ru ruthenium 44	102.9 Rh rhodium 45	106.4 Pd palladium 46	107.9 Ag silver 47	112.4 Cd cadmium 48	114.8 In indium 49	118.7 Sn tin 50	121.8 Sb antimony 51	127.6 Te tellurium 52	126.9 I iodine 53	131.3 Xe xenon 54
132.9 Cs caesium 55	137.3 Ba barium 56		138.9 La* lanthanum 57	178.5 Hf hafnium 72	180.9 Ta tantalum 73	183.8 W tungsten 74	186.2 Re rhenium 75	190.2 Os osmium 76	192.2 Ir iridium 77	195.1 Pt platinum 78	197.0 Au gold 79	200.6 Hg mercury 80	204.4 Tl thallium 81	207.2 Pb lead 82	209.0 Bi bismuth 83	[209] Po polonium 84	[210] At astatine 85	[222] Rn radon 86
[223] Fr francium 87	[226] Ra radium 88		[227] Ac* actinium 89	[261] Rf rutherfordium 104	[262] Db dubnium 105	[266] Sg seaborgium 106	[264] Bh bohrium 107	[277] Hs hassium 108	[268] Mt meitnerium 109	[271] Ds darmstadtium 110	[272] Rg roentgenium 111							

* Lanthanide series

140 Ce cerium 58	141 Pr praseodymium 59	144 Nd neodymium 60	[147] Pm promethium 61	150 Sm samarium 62	152 Eu europium 63	157 Gd gadolinium 64	159 Tb terbium 65	163 Dy dysprosium 66	165 Ho holmium 67	167 Er erbium 68	169 Tm thulium 69	173 Yb ytterbium 70	175 Lu lutetium 71

* Actinide series

232 Th thorium 90	[231] Pa protactinium 91	238 U uranium 92	[237] Np neptunium 93	[242] Pu plutonium 94	[243] Am americium 95	[247] Cm curium 96	[245] Bk berkelium 97	[251] Cf californium 98	[254] Es einsteinium 99	[253] Fm fermium 100	[256] Md mendelevium 101	[254] No nobelium 102	[257] Lr lawrencium 103

Lightning Source UK Ltd.
Milton Keynes UK
UKHW020637070521
383229UK00007B/206